DEEP WORK

*Navigating
the Psycho-Spiritual
Journey*

URI KUGEL, PHD

·

AT THE END,

NOTHING EVER HAPPENED,

NOTHING IS HAPPENING. AND

NONETHELESS, THESE WORDS

APPEAR IN A DREAM WITHIN A

DREAM.

To François

My first teacher

I am forever grateful.

CONTENTS

ACKNOWLEDGMENT

First and foremost, I would like to express my deepest gratitude to my family, whose love and support have been the foundation and core of my journey and evolution. To my wife, Lindsey, thank you for your patience, encouragement, and unwavering belief in me as I poured myself into this project. To my kids, to the endless love you have taught me. To my mother and my father, for protecting and nurturing me despite the hardships and madness that life threw your way.

To the many teachers, therapists, clients, colleagues, and friends I have had the privilege of working with in the realms of psychology and spirituality, you have been a profound source of inspiration. I am deeply grateful for the insights and experiences we've shared and honored to have walked alongside you on our journeys.

I would also like to thank the teachings of Dzogchen, Advaita Vedanta, Non-Dual Shaiva Tantra, and the healing power of psychedelic-assisted therapy, which have not only shaped this book but also profoundly transformed my life.

Finally, to the readers of *Deep Work,* thank you for embarking on this journey of self-exploration and transformation with me. May this book serve as a guide and companion as you navigate your own psycho-spiritual path.

Aho.

DISCLAIMER

Due to the largely illegal nature of many psychedelic substances described in this publication, it is important to emphasize that this book does not encourage or condone their use where it is against the law. However, the use of psychedelics occurs regardless of their legality. I believe that offering responsible harm reduction information is essential to keeping people safe. For that reason, this publication is designed to enhance the safety and efficacy for those who decide to use these substances.

Furthermore, this publication is meant as a source of information and thought stimulation for the reader. It is not meant as a substitute for direct expert assistance. If such a level of assistance is required, the services of a competent professional should be sought.

Any examples of the use of psychedelics by others were written as potential illustrations or based on given information from a participant or guide who provided such services. Lastly, any cases discussed herein do not reflect the actual identities of individuals, but a combination of factors designed to provide case illustrations. Unless otherwise indicated, all the names, characters, businesses, places, events, and incidents in this book are either the product of the author's imagination or used in a fictitious manner. Any resemblance to actual persons, living or dead, or actual events is purely coincidental.

INTRODUCTION

A S A PSYCHOLOGIST WHO HAS WORKED WITH PEOPLE FOR ABOUT twenty years, I have been personally frustrated at how slow the process of personal change can be. For most people, contemporary therapy is beneficial in preventing suicide and reducing symptoms of depression and anxiety. However, it is often just a matter of time before a relapse occurs or another set of problems emerges in an endless game of whack-a-mole. If there is one thing I have learned via my personal and professional life experience, it is that, ultimately, mental health problems and self-development stagnation are existential, rather than psychological, in nature. Eventually, we all come back to the same questions and fears: Why am I here? What happens when we die? What happens to my loved ones when they leave me? How can life be so wonderful and ruthless at the same time? Is there anyone in charge? Why does the universe exist? Is there anything outside of the universe? And so on and so forth.

Existential problems are spiritual in nature, not religious. This realization led me to explore a more integrated approach that combines psychological and spiritual practices, which I will discuss throughout this book. I define spirituality as a curious and exploratory inward gazing that does not assume a scientific paradigm of establishing a hypothesis to be validated or invalidated. Rather, it is an open perspective in which we learn from a subjective and unverifiable experience. Asking spiritual questions is as natural as children exploring the world of the imagination. Their inner and outer worlds are sandboxes, ready to be shaped by whatever arises: beauty, wonder, terror, intimacy, isolation, and love. As adults, we have moved away from this attitude into a world of conceptual boxes. We are constantly attempting to put order to the chaos that flows around us, missing out on the spontaneous patterns that appear out of total blackness.

Western civilization has made incredible advancements in technology, general medicine, and intellectual evolution. For centuries, the East has dominated the field of inner technology, such as an understanding of the mind, spirituality, and basic psychology.

Over the past 100 years or so, the western and eastern hemispheres have increasingly mingled their perspectives, influencing each other and forming a symbiotic relationship. Now, in the West, we have prominent meditation and spiritual teachers and access to scriptures and teachings that were inaccessible just a few years ago. In addition, these traditions have evolved into popular mindfulness programs, emotional intelligence, and, in some cases, the popularized use of psychedelic substances.

Unfortunately, Western culture and the medical field keep insisting, consciously and unconsciously, on separating psychology and spirituality. This trend, in my opinion, is debilitating our ability to create long-lasting changes in our mental health. More specifically, we continue to focus on addressing symptomatology and dance around existential questions without actually meeting life's core issues head-on, such as birth and death, deep trauma, the meaning of one's life, and the paradoxes that surround our existence.

There is no doubt in my mind that modern science is fundamental to global civilization and psychotherapy. However, given the recent crises that humanity is facing (e.g., climate change, geopolitical conflicts, overpopulation, pandemics, and hopelessness), there might finally be some openness and willingness to consider integrating psychology and spirituality in order to explore and understand who we are and enhance the ways we cope with the journey of life.

This can be achieved via what I call deep work, a deep journey into our soul and psyche that enables us to face our fears, shadows, and unimaginable powers. It is a journey of self-discovery and a wish for complete intimacy with oneself and the world.

Who Am I?

I was born and raised in Israel, the son of a Jewish father and a German mother who converted for my father in the early '60s. I have been searching for the truth from a young age in a journey that has taken me all around the world. I have now settled in San Diego, California.

I have been working as a therapist for over 20 years. I have a master's degree in psychology from Leiden University in the Netherlands and a PhD in clinical psychology from Palo Alto University. I have published several articles and book chapters in the field of clinical psychology. My training has taken me through classical clinical experiences in various psychiatric hospitals and outpatient settings in the US, Europe, and Israel.

My spiritual background includes 25 years of practice in various forms of tantra. I have studied with some of the most renowned contemporary Tibetan Buddhism and nondual masters in the world.

Most importantly, and similarly to many of you reading this, I was lost in trauma, pain, and suffering for significant portions of my life. Psychological interventions on their own were helpful but insufficient to relieve the pain in the long term. Therefore, the journey of unpacking my trauma and psychological development forced me to integrate psychology and spirituality in a way that was effective in liberating myself from the cycles of suffering. Over time, I have found that my process of self-development is also effective for many others. It might not fit every individual, but at the very least, I believe I have knowledge to contribute to those struggling with their mental health or in their work with others.

This book is for therapists, healers, and individuals who are interested in the process of inner evolution. I have wanted to write it for several years but struggled to put all the pieces together. It finally flowed out of me in March 2023 over a span of three weeks, following a powerful nondual Shaiva tantra retreat with Christopher Wallis. This book is not a manual or a protocol. Each person has a unique developmental puzzle that only they can complete. You cannot buy freedom. However, I wish to provide information and basic skills that could save time and prevent you from potentially stumbling into the pitfalls that I encountered.

In chapter one, "My Journey," I detail my personal evolution from a contemporary psychologist into a more holistic therapist who integrates spiritual and psychological elements into working with others.

Chapter two, "The View," describes the theoretical and spiritual orientation informing the way I work with people. This orientation relies on a set of assumptions developed from my own psychological and spiritual development.

Chapter three, "The Ego," describes in more detail the various elements and processes of the human mind. In order for us to be effective in working with our own minds and the minds of others, we need to understand the mechanics and dynamics of our inner life.

Chapter four, "The Psychic Body," focuses on the body's various elements and processes. The body-mind entity that we call a human being does not consist of separated mind and body elements but is made of a dynamic energetic system that processes thoughts, feelings, and perceptions in an efficient way. This chapter attempts to describe this system in simple terms from the perspective of a holistic, psychospiritual approach.

Chapter five, "Deep Work Foundations," dives into the skillset and areas of focus that are required to facilitate success in deep work via meditation and psychedelic therapy.

Chapter six, "Medicine," describes the benefits and potential pitfalls of working with psychedelic medicines in psychotherapeutic settings. I would like to emphasize several points regarding the work with psychedelic substances. They are unfortunately illegal in many parts of the world. However, in recent years, psychedelics have become increasingly popular in both FDA-approved studies and the underground psychedelic community. There have been hundreds of studies in this domain in recent years, and the evidence of the benefits of psychedelic-assisted psychotherapeutic approaches is becoming increasingly substantial.

Although I describe psychedelic substances in this publication, I cannot encourage or condone their use where it is against the law. However, many clients who come to my doorstep ask for advice in integrating the psychedelic experiences they already had independently of our work. Some arrive in coordination with shamanic healers and guides from the psychedelic community seeking clinical consultation. There are, unfortunately, not many clinical experts, let alone psychologists, familiar with the issues that come up in psychedelic and deep meditative experiences.

Rather than completely ignoring this important topic, I believe that offering responsible information and advice is essential to keeping people safe and promoting their healing. For that reason, this publication is aimed at enhancing the safety and efficacy for those who decide to use these substances.

Chapter seven, "Integration," focuses on the preliminary integration of insights and experiences in meditation and medicine journeys into one's identity. In addition, for those interested, this chapter describes a more advanced integration of one's identity following perceptual shifts in consciousness.

Finally, the resources section provides a list of books and programs I recommend, as I have found them to be beneficial in my own evolution.

I hope you will find the following words beneficial in your journey. Please be kind to yourself and those who cross your path in life. I ask you to use the following in benevolence and deep respect for yourself and others.

"With great power comes great responsibility." (Lee, 1962).

CHAPTER 1

MY JOURNEY

THERE IS A STORY I HEARD ONCE IN THE PSYCHEDELIC MEDICINE COMMUNITY. A group of Buddhist monks who were the entourage of a famous teacher arrived for a visit in the US. They were all very advanced meditators with many years' experience. They heard about medicine (i.e., psychedelics) work, and one of them, Tenzin, wanted to try it. Tenzin was referred to a good guide in the medicine community in the US and had an amazing spiritual experience using psilocybin mushrooms. He later told the guide that in all his previous meditations, he never got to experience the depth of union he had with the divine during his medicine journey and insights arising in his consciousness.

Tenzin could not stop raving about his experience to his friends. One of them, George, who was no less experienced than Tenzin in mindfulness meditation, was sure that the whole thing was a fraud and that Tenzin had just had a weird day. George was certain that by the power of his focus and mindfulness practice, he would not become hypnotized like his brother had. George arrived at the mushroom session with the same guide with the attitude, "I'm going to show the mushroom who is the boss around here." If you know anything about mushrooms, it's that you do not talk to them like that. Even though they are benevolent species, they are tricksters, nonetheless. The guide did their very best to create a soft and safe setting, but the session ended as an "Oh no . . . " moment. At the end of the evening, George found himself in an inpatient psychiatric unit on a hold for homicidal ideation. He took the rest of the night to calm down and eventually came back to his senses. He later shared with the guide that he was completely possessed by a demon during the experience. George returned to himself, and actually felt he had benefitted from the experience. As his hubris was highlighted, he came in contact with locked parts of his mind that needed attention, and his motivation to develop his spiritual practice grew stronger than ever.

It does not matter where you are on the political map or your ethnicity, religion, or gender. I think we can all pretty much agree that the world we are living in right now is borderline insane. We cannot deny the depths of mental, emotional, and existential hopelessness and helplessness humanity has slipped into in recent decades. Madness around us and within us. Who's driving? I have absolutely no idea. Do you?

Most people that I pass every day are doing their best to survive, make money, take care of their bodies and their family, find a way to be special and unique, and discover happiness. I do that too, but I also spend a big chunk of my time working with unhappy people. And there are so many of them!

During my PhD years, one of my professors told me once, "You're not a civilian anymore." It took a while for that to sink in. I thought I was done with the military after my time in the Israel Defense Forces (IDF), but I guess I was wrong. I think I did not really want to accept that I was now a part of the group of people who are meant to take care of the dysfunctional and injured members of our society. I have been working in mental health in the US for the last 13 years, and I can give you an inside hint of what you probably already know. Things don't look very good, on the outside or the inside.

Lack of progress in therapy, a client hitting a plateau, and relapse are some of the most common reasons for frustration and burnout among therapists in various modalities. I often felt helpless and frustrated, as I saw the same people coming back time and again.

The staff in mental health treatment settings is often very dedicated to the work with clients, and many share the feelings I had. You do not choose this career path for money or fame. Over the span of a lifetime, clinicians, nurses, and physicians go to work daily with a sense of duty and belief that they are often the last line of defense between their clients and suicidality and complete despair.

Yet, I've sat in many individual and group therapy sessions where it felt like the staff, clients, and myself were playing a game, pretending that things were going to change and traveling the same path over and over again, knowing that true change can be rare and elusive. The factors we could change were limited: a different medication, more family support, replacing the clinician, another rehab, targeting different cognitive distortions, doing another psychological assessment (only to find that the client has an undiagnosed personality disorder, so now we could prescribe a different therapeutic approach to target this new psychiatric label), and on and on.

We work with the best we've got. In public and private settings, interventions "approved" by insurance panels and state and federal agencies almost always include medications, cognitive behavioral therapy (CBT), and other behavioral approaches. These are often lifesavers and can bring significant positive change to people's lives. But in most cases (percentages vary), these interventions do not bring a significant change in a client's personality and identity. Research usually indicates that the longer the follow-up, the higher the relapse rates (Hardeveld, Spijker, De Graaf, Nolen, & Beekman, 2010).

The reason these interventions do not bring deep change to clients' lives is that they often focus almost entirely on symptomatology manifested in thoughts, feelings, and behaviors. Although these are very important facets of human reality, they are far from all-inclusive. There are deep parts of what a human being is that are not addressed by those interventions. More specifically, I am speaking about the forbidden or highly sensitive subjects in psychology and, even more so, in psychiatry, such as the "energy body," "meridians," and "chakras," not to mention "the divine" or the "soul."

I see myself as a man of science who appreciates data and verifiable information as well as logic and common sense for god's sake! But in addition, I have also stopped pretending for a while now that thoughts, feelings, behavior, and the physical body are all that we are made of. My journey to the realization that there is a lot more to us came through personal experience. It was not that I just started to believe in different ideas one day. Rather, I sought knowledge and understanding following the deep frustration I felt having worked for years as a psychotherapist and experienced continuous personal suffering in my relationship with myself and others and the deep feeling that, despite the richness of my life, it was nevertheless missing something important, something I had lost and could not find.

I ask of you not to blindly believe the words I say but to simply open yourself to the possibility that some of the things that are described in this chapter are as real as the earth you walk on. True understanding of the deeper levels of a being is only possible via personal experience.

I'd rather not go into the history of why and how the US mental health system concentrated on behavioral and, later, cognitive approaches to mental health problems. I would like to emphasize that the medical and mental health facilities in the US are excellent and full of gifted individuals at all levels of care. However, resources are often poorly used and funneled into approaches that show limited benefit. We all "know" that the healthcare and mental health systems are broken. When was the last time you tried getting an appointment with a therapist? It's also incredibly expensive if you ever want to talk to someone good who is not just doing mainstream psychology. If you have treatment-resistant depression, ten years of anxiety, or an alcohol problem, CBT and antidepressants are going to keep you alive and probably functional, but life could be so much more than just functional.

As a psychologist, I worked for years with insurance panels, often underpaid and burdened with endless administrative requirements that took as much time as I spent with my clients. The reasons for the poor conditions of these bureaucratic systems are too vast to describe and analyze here. Ultimately, they reflect the poor state of our society. Human society, not just Western or Eastern, but all of it. Mostly, it reflects that a large percentage of people on earth today are unwilling to admit and face their own darkness, helplessness, and hopelessness. We are unwilling, not due to idiocy, but because it is incredibly frightening to look deep into our nature.

A Believer

It is fun and nourishing to go to conferences, attend retreats, and have collaborative and personal relationships with other believers. I mean people who believe in love, peace, and the divine. You know the type.

Some of them are sometimes a bit too much, just like anyone else. I didn't used to be a believer. Shortly after the passing of my father, when I was twelve years old, I decided to stop believing in god. This went very well with being raised in a secular Jewish home in Israel with a German mother who had converted for my Jewish father. I could not stand the Jewish orthodoxy. I lost friends and family members to it. My friend who lived three floors above me in our tiny apartment building, someone who I grew up with from elementary to high school and into the military, just transformed overnight. He went one evening to a "lecture" and fell for it. His life was completely transformed into what appeared to be that of a cult follower. It scared me. At the time, I did not understand how someone intelligent could choose the words of scriptures and rabbis over the "real world." I chose to follow science, street smarts, and money. Now I know that there are infinite ways to the divine and ourselves. To each his own.

By my early twenties, things started to get complicated. I was afflicted by endless thinking and planning. I became more and more conscious of my rumination over different emotional difficulties (e.g., jealousy, feeling left out, being angry about not getting what I wanted, being scared of being found to be a fake, and so on). On one very troubling backpacking trip to Vietnam, I called my girlfriend. It was New Year's Eve, and I wanted to wish her a happy New Year. She was, of course, drunk and told me she had just kissed her ex-boyfriend, who also happened to have a very large penis. Things did not go very well afterward. I was in one of the most beautiful countries in the world and could not feel a thing. I was completely locked inside my mind, daydreaming about what had happened and what I was going to do or not do.

After two weeks of that torture, something inside me broke. I could not stand that my own thoughts had that much control over me. It infuriated me. I had a new goal now: to take back control of my mind. So, I returned home to Paris, made peace with my girlfriend, who would later become my first wife (the writing was on the wall, but I did not care to see it), and set out to find the one person who might be able to help.

François was a French man in his forties, old rural French aristocracy. He knew history, music, languages (i.e., Latin, French, Gaelic, English,

German, Dutch, ancient Greek, and Russian), and art. He had served in the Chasseurs Alpins, or "Alpine Hunters," French mountaineer special forces. He was a true genius and a man of many trades. There is not enough that I can say to describe him. He was really something different. I have yet to meet another person who equals him.

François was also gay and lived in a time when being gay in France was very unpopular. I do not know the extent of his suffering, but it was evident that most of us come into spirituality after life breaks us. Spirituality was his true passion, and the combination of his intelligence, eloquence, clarity, and spiritual realization was rare and sometimes felt supernatural.

He became the primary English-to-French interpreter and translator for some of the most prominent contemporary Tibetan Buddhist tantric masters in the Dzogchen (i.e., the Great Perfection) and Bonpo traditions. These included Namkhai Norbu Rinpoche, Sogyal Rinpoche (who has by now been largely canceled by the spiritual community due to reports of sexual, physical, and financial abuse), Tenzin Wangyal Rinpoche, and others. François became a close friend and teacher, and also provided me with easy access to these masters.

Until my trip to Vietnam, François was a nice friend, but when I came back to Paris, he became both my friend and root spiritual teacher. I asked him one evening in a bar in Paris, "Can you teach me to work with my mind? My thoughts are driving me crazy."

"Yes, I can," he said with a sneaky smile. "You asked for it." He then proceeded to give me a direct transmission and pointing-out instructions for the nature of mind. In a way, I only asked for directions to the bank, but he nuked me out of existence.

The nature of mind in tantric Tibetan Buddhism refers to the understanding that the most fundamental layer of reality is consciousness itself, which is what we are. Even more so, it's the entire totality of the perceived universe and reality itself as we experience it, infinitely manifested out of consciousness. So, it is basically saying that consciousness is god and that we are god, not separate from each other. This is, of course, a grossly inaccurate statement and will be misunderstood by most who do not have a spiritual practice. Moreover, it contradicts many of the most prominent spiritual streams, including certain sects of Judaism, Christianity, and Islam.

This is a lot, I know. When I began to inquire into spirituality, some of it was super interesting, and some did not make sense, like, "Why did god forget that it was god?" But I was pursuing the goal of taking control of my mind. I decided to focus on the meditations that helped me, in the beginning, to exit the train of thoughts and, later on, to discover much more.

In our first few weeks of "mind training" work, François spoke a lot about the view, the conceptual understanding of the teachings of Dzogchen. Within those talks were also direct transmissions from mind to mind about the nature of mind. At some point within the first few months, it clicked, and I had my first glimpse. While driving to a club for a night of drunk dancing, I became aware of my mind. Not just of specific thoughts but the mind itself as a field of experience. It was a small glimpse, and like an idiot, I did not bother to ask, "Wait a second! Who's watching?"

But nevertheless, it was a little spark that would grow with time and result in an avalanche of meditative experiences and a spiritual journey. I followed François around Europe from retreat to retreat, to dinners and evenings with friends, and to secret tantric practices in power places. It was an incredible period in my life, about five years of magic, friendships, and mentoring with a rare teacher in many countries as we chased traveling Tibetan masters around the world. It was a period of complete transformation from a typical Israeli into a much more open person who had Algerian friends, a Dutch girlfriend, and an apartment in Paris. A new reincarnation.

A lifetime passed. I am now 45 years old, living in the US, and happily married for the second time with two beautiful children. I have a practice that is doing well and 25 years of ongoing spiritual life. My insights and realizations have not taken even a little bit of pain from my life, but they have taken away a lot of the suffering.

Most importantly, I know, from having had several life-changing experiences, that spirituality is real. For example, I have become absolutely confident in my bones of the following and more:

1. There is something beyond the physical world that we perceive day-to-day, dimensions that we actually have access to in which there are other facets of reality.
2. Death as we think of it is not the end.
3. The brain, although amazing, is not who we are. It is a beautiful expression of what we are.
4. Reincarnation is real (in a way).
5. We are a lucid and awake part of god, simply consciousness itself, absolutely clear and transparent, glorious, perfected, and infinitely full beyond any scope of imagination.
6. The primary reason individuals are in pain is a lack of recognition of their true nature.
7. This lack of recognition is known on a deep, unconscious level.
8. This deep, unconscious knowledge attempts to surface to reveal itself to the subject.
9. This psychic movement creates tension, anxiety, and fear, often felt as an existential crisis or concerns and life's suffering.
10. The only way to address this suffering is by helping ourselves and others to facilitate this spontaneous process of self-discovery, and eventually that of our true nature.
11. Everything comes out of love.
12. The world is perfect as it is, not despite but with its imperfections, horrors, destruction, terror, and beauty. Therefore, there is no need for me to preach these insights to others. No missionary work is needed here. However, to those who come to my doorstep and ask for healing, I will offer whatever we can manifest.

In summary, I am now a believer.

Working with Others

I am not sure why exactly I was born to be a therapist. It simply turned out that way. Probably the combination of a few factors contributed: A case of complex trauma resulting from growing up in a dysfunctional family.

As a child, being a caregiver to a sick mother for a few years. Losing my father to a heart attack when I was twelve. Experiencing hearing loss due to ear tumors, which caused me to begin to read lips and people's body language to understand the essence of what they were trying to say when their audible words did not make sense. Hearing loss can be a funny thing over Shabbat dinner when someone asks you for the salt and you pass them a pickle. But at school, you are fighting for your fucking life, and you better know what people are saying or not saying to you.

I developed good people skills at a very young age and was one of those guys people always talked to. I hated it. I wanted to be in the game as a participant rather than the coach or a semi-observer. I wanted girls to want me rather than want to talk to me. It took me years to finally submit to what life had for me. Once I finally surrendered, I began to face my fears and obstacles. The process of helping others heal themselves seemed to flow through me. It is not something that I generate or hold. I am nothing, yet can manifest anything. It is liberating because "it" is not dependent on me and my imperfections, which are many. I have very little to do other than be there and love those who come to me.

As I developed spiritually and professionally, I tried many therapeutic approaches in working with people. I worked with CBT, acceptance and commitment therapy (ACT), dialectical behavioral therapy (DBT), exposure therapy, hypnotherapy, biofeedback, and eye movement desensitization and reprocessing (EMDR). I learned everything I could from anybody who was around. I cared very little about certifications and learned in the trenches for many years from gifted people doing this work.

As I was going through the process of learning to work with people and trying to achieve real change in people's lives, I learned a lot but also experienced significant frustration in how much resistance I met to genuine change. Despite my frustration, I intuitively sensed two areas of focus that called out to me. But at the time, I did not understand how to put those two together or their role in the puzzle of the bodymind and consciousness.

I knew intuitively that the relationship between therapist and client itself was the most healing factor in working with people. Now, after a long period of stewing, integration, and many mistakes, I can tell you something: the experience of deep psychological intimacy with another person enables people to become more intimate with themselves. It facilitates us to dive deeply into ourselves and discover who and what we really are. As we do so, we come to see reality as it is. This dive into ourselves and the nature of reality is what I call deep work. This book is about understanding the complexity of deep work, what factors are involved, the skills required to do it efficiently and effectively, and various tools that we can use to facilitate our journey of self-discovery and healing.

The second area that I sensed was truly important for healing and change was spirituality. I knew how important spirituality had become in my life and the power it had in changing my mind and personality from being very tight, rigid, and anxious into something lighter, more relaxed, and openhearted. But I did not know how to fuse spirituality with psychology, which at the time was a field of "science" for me and separate from the esoteric. For a while, I thought that the answer was buried in mindfulness, which was the secularized version of Buddhism picking up momentum in the San Francisco Bay Area, where I was training for my PhD in clinical psychology. For a couple of years, I attempted to approach mindfulness from the scientific perspective but was quickly disillusioned by the futility of trying to find a person in the brain, and by the rigid personality of one of my professors who "specialized" in that area.

I had two powerful experiences at the time as the universe was doing its best to point my stubborn and confused mind in the right direction. The first was a video presentation I saw of Diana Fosha, PhD, a psychologist who is known for developing accelerated experiential dynamic psychotherapy and who specializes in childhood attachment issues and trauma in adults. In the session, I watched as, within a few minutes, she brought a female client to a profound expression of emotion and intimacy with herself. I learned that emotion was an important bridge that could play a part in my journey to bring spirituality and psychology together, but I still could not figure out how.

But as stubborn as I was in not seeing, the universe was relentless in showing me a path. By the time I was licensed and started my own practice,

Lindsey, my wife, had started a new job at the Search Inside Yourself Leadership Institute (SIYLI), a nonprofit organization that sprouted out of Google in the fertile ground of thousands of software engineers deeply disconnected from emotions and stuck in their heads. The company realized they had to make a change in the psychological safety and emotional intelligence of their employees and gave the job to employee number 107, Chade-Meng Tan. Meng, equipped with a Google-sized budget, turned to neuroscientists, mindfulness teachers, and Daniel Goleman (a prominent expert in the field of emotional intelligence). A seven-week workshop was developed that quickly became a huge success in the company. It was such a success that it was eventually birthed out of Google into an independent nonprofit created to pass this workshop to high-tech companies, government agencies, the US military, banks, hospitals, and more. Even though this program was far from perfect, it was a beautiful combination of mindfulness, science, and emotion.

Lindsey strongly "suggested" I attend SIYLI teacher training. I was reluctant at the time, having spent twelve years in higher education and accumulating $120,000 in student loans. I was not excited about getting back into a learning program and increasing my debt, but if there's anyone who knows how to get me going, it's Lindsey.

So, one early morning, I found myself in a big meeting room in Hotel Kabuki in San Francisco with 80 or so other coaches, therapists, and mindfulness aficionados. Despite my initial doubts, that year-long program was life-changing for me. I continued to change and morph. Now I was a teacher, better equipped and open to public speaking, and in order to become so, I learned to go through several layers of emotional defenses, which further opened me to change.

In parallel with a process of expansion and professional development, there was another underground river flowing through me, of which I was unconscious at the time. My son was born when I was 35 and my daughter at 40. The birth of my children opened my heart and taught me that love was bigger and stronger than anything I could imagine. Maybe it was love, time at SIYLI, or just karma flowering, but something inside of me was unleashed.

The entire childhood trauma, which I thought was dust in the wind that I preferred not thinking about, started resurfacing in a game of whack-a-mole. I started smoking marijuana regularly, anxiety took hold in my body, and eventually, depression sank in. With every year my children grew older, my own childhood was reflected back to me in the perfect mirror that they are. Despite my education and experience working with others, I found myself paralyzed, unequipped and unable to take care of my problems. I was "over" regular talk psychotherapy and could not even bring myself to talk to a contemporary colleague. I was stuck on all fronts: therapy, fatherhood, marriage, and spirituality.

Once I became suicidal, I got really scared. It reminded me of my father and his ending. Around the same time, Anthony Bourdain, who was an inspirational figure for me, took his own life. It was the final straw that broke the camel's back. I was so angry and scared. I did not want my own children to go through the same process I went through. I eventually reached out to one person who I thought could maybe help. We had become friends back in PhD studies, researching together under the guiding hand of Professor Bongar. We had gone in different directions. We lost touch after graduation, and I did not know exactly what she was doing, but I knew that she was on the outskirts of psychotherapy and dabbling with psychedelics.

A phone call, a rushed reading of *How to Change Your Mind* by Michael Pollan, and a few weeks later, I found myself lying on a mat on the floor of her office in the Bay Area, having ingested a psychotherapeutic dose of MDMA.

I was finally unraveled. My body, which was my loyal guardian all these years, finally received permission to let go of all the energy, undigested emotions, fear, and anger that it held for me while I was unready and unwilling to experience and let go. In one session of medicine work with a very skilled guide (my friend), I accomplished the fruits of years of psychotherapy, which I would never have done. I owe her my life and infinite gratitude. It was a life-changing experience and the beginning of a process of deep work that took about two years of intense changes in my bodymind. Although learning and discovery never truly end, after that period, I finally arrived at a more peaceful section of the river. I could rest.

Most importantly, I now discovered and learned, in my own flesh, the missing link between spirituality and psychology. It was obviously the body, where the experience of emotions resides. The part I had been running away from for my entire life.

In my experience, the therapeutic process of healing and, most importantly, of awakening works optimally in the following stages: The person is willing to see deeply into themselves despite fear, pain, and facing the unknown. This usually happens because the individual is in so much pain that it is often a question of what feels like life and death. My own biggest shifts were always in the midst of such moments. I am usually the last guy my clients come to see. They first go to their family doctor, who gives them Prozac. Then they go to the psychiatrist, who gives them Xanax. Then they go to behavioral health services and do some CBT, maybe a detox, perhaps rehab. At this point, most individuals are still not willing to listen to the message coming from deep within them. And then some somatic (i.e., physiological) symptoms emerge: unexplained chronic pain, rashes, autoimmune disorders, migraines, allergies, and other psychosomatic presentations. Then they go to other physicians, try other meds, do more tests, get a couple of surgeries, and maybe have a dramatic suicide attempt when the tinnitus eventually drives them mad. Then they come to me. My job is easy at that point. They are willing to try almost anything, if given a ray of hope.

Once clients arrive, the work is focused on removing psychic blinders (i.e., deep psychological beliefs and misconceptions about reality) rather than convincing them to subscribe to a new belief system. There is no process of indoctrination or building a new ego identity. Rather, healing consists of destabilizing the ego in a structured and gradual manner. This can be done via several methods (e.g., guided meditations, hypnosis, breathwork, and medicine work) that are aimed at revealing reality as it is rather than maintaining or creating new conceptual layers. This process loosens psychological rigidity, reduces negative symptoms, and initiates increased intimacy with oneself and the world. This approach, which is essentially a spiritual path that also inherently includes a psychological transformation, is contrary to the mental health system's current focus on stabilizing and maintaining a functioning "healthy self-image." This work goes far beyond where the insurance companies' and federal agencies' stamp of approval would have us stop. This process is about deep work, going with our clients all the way in, as far as they are willing, leaving no stone unturned in the journey to heal, which is a journey of self-discovery and wish for complete intimacy with oneself.

Deep work is often avoided for a variety of reasons, such as these three on the client's side:

1. The lack of knowledge and experience of their deeper layers. The idea that we have unconscious elements is largely accepted conceptually, but most individuals have no experience of it, though it is right in front of us. Even most people who visit a chiropractor or an acupuncturist do not have a direct experience or sensation of energy moving in their meridians.

2. The immense fear and resistance to the deep layers. This is more relevant for people who have a history of trauma but is true for many others too. Individuals with trauma often lock away parts of their lives in order to survive, and the idea of revisiting these parts and having a relationship with them is terrifying.

3. The effort involved in deep work on the client's part is significantly larger than that of talk therapy or even spending time in a treatment facility. From my perspective, the effort is worth it all, because the alternative is a half-lived life full of anxiety, depression, substance abuse, and imprisonment in one's own mind. The effort I am talking about consists of feeling sometimes overwhelming sensations in the body, facing dark thoughts and difficult memories, and arriving at shattering insights about the nature of reality.

As a therapist, you cannot do deep work if you have not gone through the journey yourself. It is an initiation, in a way. So, you are required to overcome all of the aforementioned difficulties. Afterward, there are several additional difficulties you have to face as a therapist:

1. The fear of opening a Pandora's box. The "black box" is real. We do not know what actually lies in it or how deep it goes.
2. Guided by the principle of "do no harm," therapists often hold back from engaging in deep work, as they are not sure how the therapeutic relationship and intervention will develop. There are risks.

My deep work included a combination of spiritual seeking, psychological interventions, and medicine work (i.e., the use of psychedelics). Dzogchen liberated my mind and brought clarity into my life. Medicine work combined with meditation and guidance liberated my heart and energy body. And eventually, nondual Shaiva tantra touched all of the above, liberated my gut and my body, and allowed me to integrate all my parts into one.

There are many objections to this combination. More specifically, the use of substances is strongly discouraged by many spiritual traditions, and there truly are risks involved. Compared to most spiritual interventions (e.g., meditation, devotional practice, and so on), medicine work is more aggressive and tends to accelerate development. From an evolutionary perspective, it might be wiser for a baby to learn how to crawl well before taking up walking. Spending a significant portion of our development with meditation and psychological interventions is important. However, I cannot deny that in the last few decades, there has been a trend of acceleration in human evolution. This acceleration includes the migration of spiritual traditions from East to West and the increased use of psychedelic substances in personal and spiritual development.

I recognize that this was my path and my path alone. However, I do wish to share my experiences and understanding with others to help those who are on a similar path to draw some information and guidance. Undoubtedly, some of my teachers will disagree with me on the use of medicine for spiritual expansion. And yet, despite my love and devotion to my teachers and the traditions that carried me forth, there is an evolution in life and civilization. I cannot deny the benefit that this work has for me and for many others.

In summary, not everyone is ready or suitable for deep work. There are different levels of capacity and different levels of therapy. Each person finds their path. Eventually, all paths lead to the realization that one must go deeper into oneself to find healing and connection. If you have arrived at that place, then keep on reading. I wish you to connect with yourself and others, to find true intimacy in your life, and finally, to know the true nature of reality.

Aho.

CHAPTER 2

THE VIEW

THE TERM "VIEW" IN TANTRIC AND OTHER EASTERN SCHOOLS OF THOUGHT describes the theoretical orientation that one is required to understand in order to engage in successful spiritual practice (i.e., if you do not know where you are going, you will get lost or be easily distracted).

The following describes my view, set of assumptions, and the general theory that informs how I work with clients and my own spiritual path. In the process of developing my understanding, I drew on psychological training and personal spiritual experiences with Tibetan Buddhism, non-dual Shaiva tantra, and plant medicine (especially with los niños santos, the mushrooms). I want to emphasize that this synthesis is my perspective, which does not represent any of the aforementioned streams and teachers. Furthermore, my perspective is not superior or more accurate than any other spiritual stream. Every individual finds their own unique way and some like this one. I find that individuals who are attracted to my view are often spiritual seekers or people who came to me as a last resort because nothing else they have tried has worked (including pharmaceutical, psychological, or spiritual approaches).

This view does not bring anything new that was not said before in so many ways. However, I find that the combination described here, elements of spirituality with psychological understanding and energy work, is highly effective in liberating individuals from locked self-images and psychological blockages that stall natural evolution.

One of the first teachings I received in the Dzogchen lineage regarded the capacity of the student. According to the teaching, there are three capacity levels among students: low, average, and high. There are different interpretations of these levels, whether they are intellectual or motivational in essence. Dzogchen is viewed within Tibetan Buddhism as the highest school of tantra and appropriate for students of the highest capacity. When Namkhai Norbu began teaching Dzogchen in the West, he believed most Westerners to be of the highest capacity due to the fact that, relative to the rest of the world, significant portions of the population in Europe and the United States have a high school diploma and higher education degree. However, within a few years, Norbu found himself disillusioned with the Western mind and began insisting that his students complete at least a part of the Ngöndro, a series of lengthy practices that prepare the student's mind to receive transmissions of the nature of mind. As they take a while and require a serious commitment on the part of the student, many Westerners do their best to avoid this process and attempt to go directly to the "good stuff" (i.e., Dzogchen or Mahamudra in Tibetan tantric Buddhism and Bon).

I heard a story from Lama Lena about how her root teacher made her do the Ngöndro twice! Once she came back from her first retreat (a year-long endeavor), he took a good look at her and, with compassion, said, "Awwwww, it didn't work. Do it again."

This is not torture. This is an intervention designed to clear both the individual's mind and energy body, weaken the ego, which does not get what it wants, and develop the commitment required for this level of practice.

Similarly, it is important to recognize the level of the individual we are working with and their interest and commitment. In my case, I am interested in working with people who are of the highest capacity. To be clear, this doesn't have to do with their intelligence or worthiness but rather their *earnestness* to find the truth about themselves and reality. I am personally hungry for the truth of the nature of reality. It fills my life in all its aspects. However, many of the people I work with do not have the same level of interest. Many are interested in ameliorating their symptoms and finding peace.

An introduction to the nature of mind and medicine work is often inappropriate for people who have no or very little interest in breaking down the illusion that we call the default world. Moreover, breaking down the illusion for these individuals could be traumatic or scary and can sometimes lead to unexpected results (e.g., psychosis, manic episodes, anxiety, and depression), as their ego and identity are absolutely dependent on the maintenance of this illusion.

For such individuals, deep work begins with exploration of the psychic body, breathwork, inner-child work, and a gentle introduction to alternate states of consciousness via meditation. For most, this scope of work will be sufficient to address many of their psychological symptoms and send them on their path with a greater feeling of peace. However, their suffering will not end because of the fundamental lack of recognition of their true nature and the nature of reality. They will come back or find another modality that will facilitate their journey in a manner appropriate for them. However, some of these individuals will experience an ignition of the spiritual instinct and will be ready to ask to deepen the work. This interest indicates that these individuals are of the highest capacity and should be given great attention and dedication. Each one of them will touch the lives of thousands, spreading the truth and easing the suffering of others.

True Nature

The fundamental assumption in this view asserts that the primary reason that humans suffer is spiritual and existential in nature. More specifically, due to a basic misunderstanding, we have forgotten our true nature and become hypnotized by the content of reality and lost in the universe. We have fallen asleep and are dreaming a dream that never happened. To compare this to major dogma, we can think about the departure of Adam and Eve from the Garden of Eden. They were originally united with god, but then something happened, and they left that reality and became separated from the divine.

I will further unpack this statement, but first, it's important to understand that language and conceptualization are incapable of describing our true nature, as it is nondual. In the same way, English or any other spoken language cannot accurately describe quantum reality. The most we can do is use mathematics to point at the principles of that reality.

To point a finger in the right direction, we must use language. Language can only describe some of the principles of our true nature, but it will never be accurate or give an actual sense, feeling, or true understanding of our reality. There is no way to comprehend conceptually how a misunderstanding of our true nature can occur; we must *experience* a state of nonduality.

Please, do not just believe the words I say. Judge for yourself based on experiences rather than dogma or conceptual explanations.

According to this view, our true nature is a living being, a part of the whole, the divine, never separated from the totality of the universe. Our true nature is ultimate and naked consciousness, which is both the creator, the fabric of creation, all matter, all energy, and that which experiences it all. The experiencer is also capable of self-division into many sets of eyes (i.e., all sentient beings in the universe) that enable its self-experience within and out of infinite perspectives.

In reality, we have never shifted an inch or existed for a split second. Time exists merely as a conceptual construct in a universe that manifests "inside" ourselves. Simulation theory (i.e., the idea that we live in a simulated universe) comes close to describing aspects of this reality but doesn't fully capture it. Using simulation theory as an analogy, we could say that the simulation, everything that takes place "inside" the simulation, the "computer" itself that generates the simulation, and the operator of the simulator are all one. The One.

Suffering

Our initial misunderstanding and the temporary forgetfulness of our true nature causes us to believe in a separate self and mark the beginning of this belief in a separate self-image. The essence of a self-image is the deep core belief that we are each only an individual, separated from the whole, living in an ever-shifting universe at the mercy of chaos and endless cycles of birth and death, a prison of suffering from a limited perspective.

Furthermore, as an individual believing itself to be separated from the whole, we experience three major types of suffering (according to Buddha Shakyamuni):

1. The suffering of suffering—all forms of physical and emotional pain, illness, aging, and dying. This includes the fear of dying, the fear of being sick, etc.

2. The suffering of change—remember a beautiful sunset you saw and the sneaky contraction as you knew it was about to end. As Lama Lena says, "Impermanence is a bitch!" (Lena, 2018) The universe is in constant dynamic flux. Stars are born and die, furniture disintegrates over time, bodies age and get wrinkly and saggy, our sexual impulses diminish, our personalities change, people change. My son and daughter have both told me so many times they would like to stay children forever because "It's so much fun!" as they throw their little bodies at me, stepping on my face yet showering me with endless love. That too shall pass.

3. The suffering of human existence—we know. Deep down, we know, as we are god itself, fragments of god, yet still god itself. As your tiny little DNA contains the instructions for the entire human body, so does your little human being contain god itself within it. It's incomprehensible, and not so many years ago, this statement would have landed me on a nice warm pyre or the cross. Because we know; there is a gnawing feeling in our soul and our body, a daily reminder of something "not right," something incomplete, something missing, that pushes us to search. Initially, we will search "outside" for that missing thing: cars, money, sex, power, etc. Eventually, and usually following significant pain and suffering, our search will move inside.

Self-Images and Samskaras

While going through life, our identities and self-images continuously change. Whether in one life or in many, we record our identities in an infinite storage machine that we call the psychic body (i.e., energy body). In addition to these recorded self-images are undigested emotional experiences (called *samskaras* in Sanskrit) that were too overwhelming to be fully experienced during their initial manifestation and thus remained fully or partially stuck in our system.

For example, a child experiences great fear while lying in bed at night and witnessing the dark. If the child has no available parent to assist with processing the fear, the mind will eventually distract the child and package this unresolved emotional movement into a deposit that gets stored for another occasion when maturity and additional support will be available to fully digest this experience.

Samskaras do not need to arrive from extremely traumatic events. They are often created by trauma, but everything is relative. Essentially, any emotional experience that was too overwhelming for us to experience fully at any stage of development will leave a residue that spontaneously wants to release when circumstances are ripe. For a more in-depth discussion of this process from a medical-psychological perspective, I highly recommend reading *The Body Keeps the Score* by Bessel van der Kolk.

Samskaras are, in some ways, living energy entities that attempt to release themselves and unite back with the source energy they came from. However, as humans unaware of our true nature, we experience this process as psychological problems, self-hate, grandiosity, and bodily aches and pains. Eventually, if we really don't get the message, we will fall ill, and finally, death will liberate us, giving us another chance with a new body with the best possible circumstances for releasing these knots in our soul.

The Path

The term "path" refers to the plan of action. How are we going to address our current state of subjective separation from the divine and the suffering that results?

The path is simple and straightforward according to Dzogchen's root teacher, Garab Dorje:

1. Be introduced to the nature of mind—have a direct, vivid, and visceral experience of your true nature.
2. Decide upon one thing, and one thing only—see your nature, feel your nature, and be your nature in all states, at all times.

3. Have absolute trust in your nature—know always beyond any doubt, with your ultimate authority, that you are your nature and that all that manifests is your nature.

Dzogchen says that for a person of the highest capacity, hearing this instruction will suffice, and they will experience an immediate awakening that will never fall. This is very rare, but it happens. In modern times, Eckhart Tolle is a good example. Without much spiritual practice, to my knowledge, following intense ripening, he experienced a spontaneous awakening that never left him.

For most others, myself included, awakening is a gradual process of "I got it. I lost it." There will usually be an initial glimpse (stage one, per Garab Dorje) and a lot of time spent buzzing around stages two and three with some long periods of forgetting our nature along the way. This will last until the final belief that one exists will blow out like a candle flame. When the seeker disappears, there is no more problem. The world, as it is, is already perfect.

Please do not get the idea at this point that the goal of the path is to kill or get rid of the ego. Some spiritual streams absolutely set this as a goal, but according to my understanding and experience, there is no problem with the ego, only in the belief that *you* are the ego.

Spiritual streams and major religions have various ways of advising individuals to progress on the path. Some paths are super regimented and strict (e.g., Conservative Judaism) and some super loose (e.g., San Francisco Buddhism). I have followed a wide range of approaches over the span of 25 years. Each has its advantages and pitfalls. My path has culminated in tantra, the weaving of the divine and this world, but it remains only one of many. Your path is yours alone. Neither your child nor the love of your life can take your path. You might all be going to the same teacher or church, yet each is "alone" within their mind and has a unique experience of reality. I urge you to seek and find your way, for this life is more precious than you can possibly imagine.

However, some cautious advice from the lips of Jesus Christ in the Gospel of Thomas: "Let him who seeks continue seeking until he finds. When he finds, he will become troubled. When he becomes troubled, he will be astonished, and he will rule over the All." Patterson, Robinson, & Meyer, 1998)

It is often the case that initial awakening can result in being "troubled." The world as we know it has now been transformed and our perspective on reality changed. This will impact our values, relationships, and beliefs. It can be quite a shock for many individuals, and as exciting and positive as the change might be, it can also bring fear and grief in letting go of old structures and parts of our identity. I highly recommend Adyashanti's *The End of Your World* as a companion to this process. Adyashanti went through the same process throughout his awakening, and I find his examples very helpful for others who are likely to struggle with similar difficulties in their evolution.

The Role of Guides and Therapists

For guides and therapists who might ascribe to this view, your initial role is to help individuals awaken to their true nature. Some clients arrive with initial experiences of awakening, as was my case following intense meditation retreats. Some clients will experience their initial awakening (called *bodhi* in Sanskrit) with our help via work with plant medicines or other techniques (e.g., deep meditative states, hypnosis, or breathwork) that induce extra-conscious states.

The process of awakening is gradual for most individuals. We become aware of our true nature and understand that all self-images are illusory and empty because they are simply not who we truly are. Most people, after initial awakening, find self-images and samskaras present and "locked" in various locations in their physical body, energy body, and unconsciousness. Self-images in particular have a strong self-preservation force and, due to momentum and habit (i.e., *karma*), we become hypnotized by them and believe in them again and again.

Ultimately, the path is the process of liberation (i.e., *moksha*), of clearing these false self-images by seeing them for what they are and processing undigested emotions by experiencing them. This enables us to live life as it is, becoming more and more identified with our true nature, not out of belief but from experiences that erase all doubts.

As therapists and guides, I see the essence of our work as helping people who are stuck with particular self-images and samskaras that induce tremendous pain and prevent them from fully knowing themselves. We have experience and tools to help our clients liberate themselves from these blockages.

However, self-images and samskaras are almost infinite. We have forgotten ourselves for a very long time. The release of self-images and samskaras is not enough. In order to live an awakened life, immersion in and identification with our true nature are essential. Otherwise, additional self-images and samskaras will resurface and cause awareness to fixate upon these, causing a new cycle of suffering. Many clients and colleagues I know get fixated for many years on discovering these samskaras and self-images. Although this part of the journey is essential, at some point, it will be time to put down your mochila (backpack) and return home.

In summary, following the initial awakening and lessening of self-images and samskaras, the focus should shift to realizing our true nature again and again, becoming more confident in who we truly are, and allowing life to flow through us with absolute freedom.

The path I'm suggesting is not dogma. It involves focusing time, attention, and intention on several domains. In my opinion, there is only one requirement for any of this to work, which is the willingness to let go of ideas and beliefs and begin to trust your subjective experience of reality as you discover yourself. If you've read so far, then I suppose you're willing to leave ideas behind. Remember, the path of consciousness expansion is that of subjective experience and discovering your ultimate authority.

This path is about self-discovery and self-realization. That is, truly understanding who and what you are. This journey of self-discovery is unique to each person. The following is nothing but accounts of others actively walking this path, sometimes against their conscious wishes but due to a relentless need. You might find something in here that could assist you further on. There is no right or wrong way of taking this journey. In essence, it is about full intimacy with yourself and the world.

Medicine and Spiritual Work

It is noteworthy that many spiritual teachers from various streams dissuade students from the use of psychedelics. Ram Dass's guru Neem Karoli Baba said, "These medicines will allow you to come and visit Christ, but you can only stay two hours. Then you have to leave again. This is not the true samadhi. It's better to become Christ than to visit him, but even the visit of a saint for a moment is useful . . . . But love is the most powerful medicine." (Neem Karoli Baba, n.d.)

Ram Dass summarizes his opinion in a blog post about psychedelics: "How many times will you try to get high hoping that this time you won't come down—until you already know as you start to go up that you will come down? The down is part of the high. When in meditation you are tempted by another taste of honey, your memory of the finiteness of those moments tempers your desire. More bliss, more rapture, more ecstasy—just part of the passing show. The moment in its fullness includes both high and low and yet it is beyond both." (Dass, n.d.)

In contrast, for many indigenous populations around the world that lived in relative harmony with nature, the use of entheogen teachers (e.g., mushrooms, cacti, toad poison, ayahuasca brew, etc.) was a normal and natural part of their spiritual path. These teachers came to me in times of my own great need, and I cannot express the immensity of the gratitude that I have for the experiential teachings, energetic healing, and introductions to ultradimensions of reality that I received from these nonhuman teachers. There is no doubt that I am colored by my experiences and yet feel that it is an important direction to examine, especially given recent compelling data about the benefits of MDMA and psilocybin treatments for various mental health conditions.

Based on my experience, I think that psychedelic medicines can be used when appropriate for two primary purposes:

1. Psychotherapeutic purposes—psychedelic medicines are potent tools that can increase intimacy with oneself and others. They are wonderful at removing stuck energy and releasing samskaras from

the psyche (i.e., the psychic body). They confront our rigidity, need for control, and hidden and avoided emotions. Psychedelics are wonderful for trauma work, anxiety, and depression. This work requires a brave practitioner who has done work themselves and has the capacity to witness the most beautiful and darkest sides of humanity. It's not for the fainthearted, but using psychedelic medicines in safe and intentional settings focused on personal and interpersonal growth can bring amazing change into people's lives. I have seen many such results.

2. Spiritual growth—psychedelics by themselves are generally insufficient for achieving total and abiding awakening. However, they are still very beneficial in the process if used appropriately for the following reasons:

    a. Most importantly, at the very least, all organic entheogens have spirits and are, therefore, teachers. They don't speak human or in words. They use archetypal language, somatic activation, and synesthesia to communicate. Their understanding of the true nature of reality is profoundly more expanded than our current human civilization. These teachers are benevolent. They can be very aggressive in their work but ultimately teach love and intimacy with oneself and the universe. A proper medicine session often ends in a feeling of awe for the power of these teachers.

    b. Most people on the spiritual path can have massive breakthroughs initially but will then get stuck due to fear or other repressed psychological barriers. Psychotherapeutic work can remove some of these blocks and allow awakening to move more rapidly.

    c. These medicines transmute and move energy from stuck samskaras.

    d. There is an ability to reaffirm meditative states, insights, and experiences of awakening in the amplified state induced by psychedelics. This increases our subjective authority over our general state of being.

However, a word of caution regarding the use of entheogenic teachers: they are not for everyone. They are extremely powerful, and sometimes their teachings can overwhelm an unprepared human mind and body. It is important to use them appropriately and safely.

Combined with a solid spiritual foundation, they can lead to massive change. For each individual, we need to weigh the risk of any particular medicine versus the potential benefit. For example, I would not generally recommend ibogaine (an entheogenic plant agent originating in Africa) as an integral part of the path of spirituality. But for Mia, a heroin addict, it was a lifesaver. Meditation, mantra recitation, bodywork, and hypnosis were insufficient to keep her away from heroin. She went through over 20 rehab facilities in her struggle with this addiction, which decimated her body and relationships with others. One ibogaine treatment was enough to put that war to rest and give her a rebirth into a new life with new opportunities. However, I would not take it unless I had no choice. That is not my path.

At the end of the day, any path can be dangerous, as the final interpretation and integration lies with the student. You can take a psychedelic to find your nature and become psychologically dependent on it, or you can become dependent on a meditation technique to arrive there. Remember that the origin of suffering lies in misunderstanding and misperception. That is an ongoing process, since we interpret reality to be other than what it is.

Following a powerful unity-consciousness experience (resulting from meditation or medicine), one could decide to jump off the roof, as they concluded that their body is no more "real" than anything else. Yet, let me assure you, if you ever jump off the roof, you are unlikely to transform into rainbow light, and you will break your poor bones or worse.

The Fruit

At some point, and usually gradually, the path turns into the fruit. Once we stop believing ourselves to be separate from the whole, we are liberated to experience life fully, as we become less and less identified with self-images and our separated, immediately present body. We no longer resist experiencing the entire spectrum of life: sadness, grief, anger, fear, love, joy, and bliss. Every possible experience is allowed; they all have an underlying taste of consciousness itself. This is total and absolute freedom.

As this process unfolds, we come to understand that all experiences are a form of divine expression, manifesting itself through our unique set of eyes, body, and personality. This is *pogha* (i.e., embodiment). We are both an embodiment of the divine and an inseparable part of it, and we will be fully united with it at the end of the body we wear for this life.

Many spiritual paths aim for transcendence and, therefore, take us away from the physical world. For example, there are many meditators who focus on remaining in a state of *samadhi* (i.e., absorption) in deep meditative states and thus escaping the world of physicality and form. In addition, the major religions (i.e., Islam, Christianity, and Judaism) promote worship in this life so that in the "next life" (or heaven), we will achieve liberation and taste the fruit of our work.

This path is about first discovering our transcendent aspects (i.e., our true nature) and then bringing them down to our body and earth and discovering that the world itself is our true nature. There is no time, in the future or elsewhere, when we will taste the fruit. It is now, in this life, in this body, where the story completes itself.

In addition, there is an unfolding mystery, forever filling us with passion, devotion, and curiosity for how much more we can see into and realize our nature and the beloved. There is no limit to how deep we can go into our true nature. The deeper we go, the more it opens up.

It is nearly impossible to describe the reality of a person who has completed this process and tasted the full fruit. A person coming from the world of dualism (i.e., dead vs. alive, black vs. white, good vs. evil, etc.) believes and perceives themselves as moving through a world that is "out there." The center of such a world is "my body" and the center of the body is the brain, where the mind is supposedly located according to medical and behavioral science.

When we discover and begin to somatically experience nondual consciousness (i.e., there is nothing but consciousness and everything that we see appears "in it as it"), we come closer to the perspective of tantra.

Our experiences are now understood as made from us, coming from us, reflecting us, and dissolving back into us. We now experience ourselves as an infinite, dynamic, and perfect being engaged in a cosmic game in which love is the only reality. We are not moving through anything, but everything moves through us. As Nisargadatta Maharaj taught, "Wisdom tells me I am nothing. Love tells me I am everything. And between the two my life flows." (Nisargadatta Maharaj, 1973)

Terms

Before moving on, let's define some terms that I will be using throughout this book:

MEDICINE—this term usually refers to the use of psychedelics, which are entheogenic agents or several synthesized molecules. More specifically, I speak about cannabis (i.e., marijuana), MDMA (i.e., Molly, ecstasy), psilocybin (i.e., los niños santos, the holy children), DMT (often derived from ayahuasca, which is frequently referred to in the psychedelic community as the Grandmother), 5-MeO-DMT (which is a particular type of DMT produced in nature by toads, therefore this medicine is also known as the Toad), mescaline (often derived from peyote and San Pedro cacti and referred to as the Grandfather), ibogaine, LSD, 2C-B, and more.

CEREMONY—the occasion when the use of medicine occurs. Ceremony is commonly used as a term in shamanic settings and often but not only in group sessions.

JOURNEY—a psychedelic experience, often involving the use of medicine but can also be induced using other techniques such as drumming or breathwork.

JOURNEY SPACE or MEDICINE SPACE—the energetic field that takes place in a specific location (e.g., room, yurt, tent, sweat lodge, etc.) that often involves the use of medicine but could also be dedicated to other interventions (e.g., breathwork, drumming, etc.). Guides often believe and work under the assumption that the physical space in which ceremonies and deep work occur accumulates energy and thus has an effect of its own. Therefore, the location of the work is important and often involves the use of crystals and other tools that can amplify the effects of the intervention and medicine.

MEDITATION—refers to various practices that work with faculties of the mind, attention, imagination, and inner work. Essentially, working with the mind-body system, tinkering with the OS (operating system) itself, and using various interfaces.

INTIMACY—is about the ability to become very close with ourselves, our experience, and others. Intimacy is not sex, although sex can be intimate. Intimacy is about wanting to be with yourself, the world, or someone else without holding back or protecting yourself with defenses, pretensions, or bracing. To be emotionally and psychologically naked and fully embrace life as it comes your way.

THE VEIL—The veil is the barrier between consciousness and the unconscious. In waking life, you do not experience hallucinations, you do not dream. If you were to experience hallucinations during waking hours, we could say you were psychotic. The veil has a function. It isolates us from the full potential of the unconscious and allows us to focus on physical reality. At night, while sleeping, the ego defenses are down, as is the veil to some extent, allowing material from the unconscious to come into our conscious experience.

CHAPTER 3

EGO

PHILOSOPHERS, PSYCHOLOGISTS, AND SPIRITUAL PRACTITIONERS HAVE attempted to analyze and conceptualize the human mind for thousands of years. This chapter synthesizes ideas and insights I have learned over the years via meditation, studying scriptures, and my own medicine journeys. I wrote it in the context of understanding the different elements of the mind pertaining to deep work and people's wish to change. I introduce the mind's elements, processes, and how it shows up in various psychological states that I often see in my practice. I named this chapter "Ego," as, in essence, the primary problem with the human mind is the compulsive process of identifying with its contents, which is the basis of egoic identity.

Constructing the Ego: Thoughts

Andy, a 17-year-old, walked into the office and sat down heavily on the blue velvet couch. He said, "I'm not gonna get an A+ in history."

"I'm sorry to hear that," I said.

His face turned sunken and dark. He continued, "If I don't get an A+, I'm not going to get into that school."

I asked, "And then?"

"Then it's the end!" His eyes turned big and his face red. "Then I'm not going to be successful for sure," he said, calming down as he surrendered to that belief.

I asked, "Who said you need to be successful?"

He looked at me, surprised, scratching his chin with a confused expression on his face.

It can be a good thing for a therapist when their clients become confused.

Confusion is often used in hypnosis. Turns out that people are significantly more suggestible to instructions and guidance when confused. Our defenses are down, and so, we better accept reality as it is presented to us.

But presented by whom? By what? We ordinarily believe that we produce our thoughts and feelings. However, if you meditate, you will eventually arrive at the experience that thoughts emerge in the back of your mind without your having any control over them. Can you find the event horizon at the edge of your consciousness? Can you find the origin of thoughts and the place where they dissolve? Ultimately, the mind is a conceptual machine, creating abstract boxes around any perceived inner and outer phenomena. Just for a while, can you let go of the concepts you have of what the ego is? Forget for a few minutes all you have learned about this entity. Put these ideas in a black box and open yourself to your subjective and immediate experience. Now. Investigate for yourself, via your subjective and immediate experience.

What is a thought, in your subjective experience? Forget about neurology, the brain, and science for a few minutes. We aren't invalidating them, only putting them aside ("bracketing" them) for a minute to examine reality from our immediate experience. Do you like chocolate? Do you like raw onions? How do you know? It is a matter of immediate authority. You instantly know whether you like them or not. Similarly, with the same authority, examine your immediate reality. Can you find a thought? When you look at it, what happens to it?

Have you ever asked yourself where thoughts come from? Isn't it amazing? You are just going about your day and, all of a sudden, an urge to stuff something into your mouth comes up. A thought arises—"I'd like a snack." And there you go, like a robotic slave, following that thought and getting a snack. This is followed by infatuation ("Yum yum. Life is good") or guilt ("I really shouldn't have eaten that"). Or maybe you start arguing with yourself ("No! You don't need a snack. Get some self-control. What about your goals? What about your health?"). Like a person hypnotized by a news item ("Gas prices on the rise!"), we follow an initial thought into a full-blown dramatic scene. This scenario is simple enough to handle, but what about when other people get involved? Sometimes you might just have a thought about saying "hi" to someone on the street and then you just say "hi" or walk around arguing with yourself why you said or didn't say "hi." What does this all mean about you?

If you meditate, which I highly suggest you do, you will eventually discover something. However, having me tell you what that is won't change a thing, because what is required is a perceptual shift, a visceral experience and an Aha! moment of understanding that comes from "seeing" rather than thinking.

So, go "see" for yourself that, in our subjective experience, we do not know where thoughts come from. When you meditate with your eyes closed, or open, as is often done in Dzogchen Semde, you will see thoughts arise, hang out for some time, and then dissolve. Then you will begin to notice that there is a space in between or around the thoughts, a psychic space, absolutely transparent and immeasurable in any way. For some, it's a subjective feeling of emptiness, void. This feeling of emptiness and void is actually quite common. For example, the first moments when you wake up in the morning and the mind hasn't started to talk (if you're lucky and living a calm life). However, even though we experience it so often, we do not notice it consciously. We're not aware of this seemingly transparent and unimportant space.

Pick one object in the room you're in right now, any object. Now, become more fully aware of it. Focus your attention on this object and notice all the things you haven't noticed before: the reflection of the light, the dents in the texture, the texture itself, the feeling tone of the object, how hot or cold it is, and how much you like or dislike it. Notice the richness of the experience. Similarly, in meditation, and later at all times, noticing awareness itself reveals its qualities and characteristics. The more you "look," the more god opens itself to itself as you.

It is glorious if you think about it. God plays hide and seek with itself. God placed secret doors to itself among all the holographic objects of creation. The one "thing" that is common to all these doors and the one key to them all is One: awareness. For if it is not in awareness, it is not in existence.

If you dive deeper into the experience of emptiness from which thoughts emerge, your experience of it will grow and several perceptual shifts are likely to occur. Ultimately, you will arrive at the Ground of Being.

Thoughts are continuously generated in the space of open awareness, or the ground of consciousness, often referred to in spiritual language as the Ground of Being, Shiva, or the Supreme Source (usually depicted as a male force or entity). Anything I say here is nothing but a pointer; I can't actually convey the experience because it is nondual. Thoughts are not generated in the ground of being but appear out of it, like a fountain of sparkles of light appearing out of black velvet emptiness and then falling back into it.

One of the teachings in nondual Shaiva tantra that I find very beneficial is the teaching about the five acts of the divine. This is often depicted by a statue of Shiva that shows his hands and feet in various positions symbolizing the five acts, which are: 1) creation, 2) stasis of creation, 3) dissolution of creation, 4) concealment of the divine, and 5) revealing the divine. If we apply this algorithm to the life of a thought, it will look as follows:

1. Creation—a thought is born in your mind, appearing out of the ground, the absolute and total velvety darkness.

2. Stasis—the thought hangs for a while, slows down enough for you to watch it, experience it, savor it, and maybe give it enough attention and develop it further into a train of thoughts, action, and emotion. You can record and remember it.

3. Dissolution—now the thought begins to fade, like when you wake up from a dream in the morning and it fades away, no matter what. As this starts, you know it's leaving, like fog disappears with the rays of the sun.

4. Concealment—there is no self-awareness. There is absolute absorption into the thought. You do not notice that you are thinking but completely follow the thought, like being absorbed in the movie, not remembering you're sitting in a movie theater.

5. Revelation—for whatever reason, you become self-aware. You notice, "I am thinking." You are aware of the "I." Understand that, as far as we know, we are the only species that can at least say that. For most people, this ends with self-awareness of the I as the ego. Hence, you become aware of yourself as the subject of a thought,

but that is immediately translated into more thoughts about your-self, descriptions of yourself, etc. However, for the awakening process, each moment of self-awareness is an opportunity to truly become aware of your true self and aware of your awareness.

The movement of thoughts is often referred to in tantric traditions as Shakti, power, or energy. Shakti is usually depicted as a female/goddess energy and deity. Shakti essentially manifests according to tantra, the entire inner and outer world. Hence, all thoughts, feelings, sensations, and all the objects you see—cars, people, roads, animals, skies, stars, and so on—are something like holographic radiation (the radiation being Shakti) coming out of the ground of being into itself. And the ground of being is itself con-sciousness, often referred to as Siva. Siva and Shakti are not separate. They are one, two aspects of the one.

Self and Ego

The ego is a machine. Now, please remember everything I say is an approximation. The ego doesn't really exist, it only appears to exist. I love Adyashanti's suggestion to see the ego as a verb rather than an object or noun. As a verb, the primary function of the ego is that of appropriation. What happens in our field of experience is appropriated into our identity. For example, if you see a flower, thoughts will arise that dictate how you relate to this flower: "I love it," "I hate it," "I need more flowers at home," "I should buy more flowers for my wife," "Nobody buys flowers for me," and so on.

If thoughts are particles, the ego is like the force of gravity pulling them all together. The force of gravity is a continuous process of self-appropria-tion. Imagine a planet being born in space. First, there was one particle. The mother particle. The first little piece of dirt.

For us, that first particle was a very simple feeling of "Me." It is a somatic feeling, very unique, and yet difficult to describe and localize without deep meditative or psychedelic experiences. Sometimes it can also be difficult to sense because for most people it is covered under mountains and freeways of thoughts, plans, goals, checklists, fears, and fantasies.

I can feel my basic feeling of "me;" this "Uri" feeling is palpable. I cannot describe it and have no idea if it is unique to me or similar to yours. If you pay attention to it, you might be able to sense it. The essence of this original particle is "I."

Then a second particle appeared in our consciousness. This one is called *sensation* or *perception*. Now you have a conscious being that experiences sensations and perceptions. A small infant, a few days old, has no language, no information about what is happening, no capacity to even describe oneself or be self-aware. There is a feeling of aliveness and now also of sensation.

As the infant becomes aware of the sensation of their feet, head, stomach, and soiled bottom, they begin to differentiate between comfortable and uncomfortable sensations. They also begin, over time, to notice a relationship of cause and effect between sensations and the world. I'm uncomfortable in my tummy, crying for food. The ego's first unspoken statement is "I'm alive!" which is the subject. The second statement is "I sense!" which is the object. And the third statement is the essence of suffering, a complete unspoken statement, "I lack something" (e.g., milk, love, touch, comfort, etc.). Here you can see the linear universe in which the ego operates, in which subject relates to object:

"I need something."

"I want something."

"What would happen to me?"

"I love you."

"I hate you."

"I am too fat."

"I am poor."

"I am pretty."

And so on and so forth.

The ego is a force of gravity that pulls many thoughts and perception particles together. Over time, they form a crystalized structure that will, at some threshold (usually between 15 and 18 months old), become self-aware. As language develops and matures, this simple self-awareness turns into an identity.

Now, from the unawakened perspective, life is not simple. The ego has a nemesis called chaos, also known as impermanence. Lama Lena once said something that cracked me up, as it was so painfully true: "Impermanence is a bitch" (Lena, 2018). The continuous and endless dynamic flow of the universe causes everything to appear, maintain, and then dissolve. Give it enough time and pressure, and eventually all parts of the crystalized mass of what a human identity is made of will expire and fade away. We get a job, we lose a job. We have friends, then they change, and friendships fall apart. We get money, we lose it. We manifest beauty, but our face and body change. The weather changes. Everything is constantly changing, and the ego has to work very hard to keep things crystallized. Yet, it cannot help itself because it is fulfilling its purpose. It is a house of cards destined to eventually fall apart. It is built around a hollow center that, deep down, knows itself to be absolutely empty. From the unawakened perspective, it terrifies us.

The ego also has a name. It's your name. The ego likes itself or it hates itself. As long as it is engaged in a process of self-reference, it doesn't really matter. As long as the process keeps this house of cards erect, it matters not what the particles are made of. Gravity will pull into itself any type of matter with no discernment. For example, negative thoughts and images pull on other negative thoughts and perceptions, and that crystallization of thoughts quickly becomes beliefs and then a negative self. Or positive thoughts pull on other thoughts and create a narcissistic personality.

The process of engagement in self-referencing creates further reasons to justify this identity. In its center, there is an absolute, empty, open presence, but it appears hidden from view by a story of "me." There is the history of the stuff that happened to me, how it happened, and why it happened. Poor me and poor them. I fucking hate myself or I fucking love myself. Fuck the world; save the planet (i.e., "I" must save the planet).

Ego Defenses

The ego not only builds itself; it also protects itself. It has self-preservation instincts much like our immune system, mostly because it likes the status quo, equating this with safety. It doesn't like when particles fly off in different directions. This is an instinct. We don't "decide" to explode in anger when someone cuts us off on the freeway or gives us criticism. It just comes flying out of us.

The ultimate goal of the ego is to preserve itself, the "me" story. This also includes the survival of the physical body. It has ways to go about this that we call ego defenses: these are processes that form as instinctive responses to events that threaten our integrity. The primary purpose is to protect us by solidifying an identity around a new narrative. The ego gets responses to its defenses from the environment. Negative or positive doesn't matter; as long as there is a subject-object relationship, the subject is reinforced. Here are some examples:

> *Anger*—one of the most common forms of ego defense. It is directed at others who threaten the ego structure. Its essence is blame: "You did this to *me*."
>
> *Fear*—when your physical or emotional integrity is threatened, fear is often a first response, although many people, especially men, are allergic to this emotion, so it is usually covered with anger in our culture.
>
> *Guilt*—something we did had an unpredictable or negative effect on our life. A child feeling guilty for drawing on the wall. The guilt creates a new narrative, "I'm bad," to which the parents now have to respond.
>
> *Shame*—another version of "there is something wrong with me." Although embarrassment is a normal biological response designed to protect young offspring from strangers, shame is a complicated cognitive and emotional process that is all about identity.

The Unconscious to Conscious Spectrum

Consciousness is quite clear: it is everything that you are aware of at any given time. It shifts, as there is a limit to how much you can be conscious of. Can you notice your left little toe? Now you can, but as you have done so, you are no longer conscious of the back of your head. The ego operates mostly in the unconscious. What we actually experience in consciousness is nothing but the tip of the iceberg.

I was trained in hypnotherapy by Edwin (Ed) Yager, whom I met early in my career in San Diego. When I met Ed, he was a handsome, 90-year-old man. He was a licensed clinical psychologist who switched careers at 50 years old, from a structural engineer to a psychologist, following a life-changing hypnotic entertainment presentation he attended. I had two years with Ed before he passed away at 92, and I see him as an inspirational example of aging. He dedicated a massive portion of his life to working with and helping others, yet seemed to always be full of energy and savoring life as it came his way with no hesitation. I highly recommend his book *Foundations of Clinical Hypnosis: From Theory to Practice* if you are interested in acquiring a powerful tool for working with others.

One of the first demonstrations that Ed gave me was the introduction of the unconscious. It is obvious that a very large aspect of a human being is unconscious, yet we often need a pointing-out instruction to appreciate the magnitude and power of our unconsciousness.

So, hear me out if you've never thought about it before. As you read these words, your heart is pumping blood, your lungs breathe, your brain is processing an immense multitude of neurological signals coming from 100 billion neurons, your endocrine system is releasing hormones, your liver is cleansing your blood, your digestive system is . . . digesting, and your immune system is fighting billions of bacteria and viruses in your skin, guts, blood, and airways. Almost the entirety of these processes is done unconsciously. We can actually say that the majority of human functioning is unconscious.

Furthermore, look around yourself right now. Everything you perceive, sights, odors, sounds, temperatures, and the feeling of the clothes on your body, are all processed in your brain (according to modern science) and presented to you as a final polished, cohesive product. If you study a bit more about neuroscience and the processing of sensory information, you will come to realize that what you perceive is actually very different from what we call objective reality. (There are several spiritual and scientific approaches that deny the existence of objective reality instead of arguing that perception is subjective and often faulty).

For example, there is a delay of several dozen milliseconds between light hitting your retina and the signal arriving at the brain, and about 120 milliseconds before you can actually take action based on what you see. In addition, your thoughts, beliefs, and expectations all influence what and how you perceive information coming from the senses. For example, someone with war-related PTSD could instinctively interpret the sound of a backfired car as a gunshot. Their body will react very differently than someone without these patterns of interpretation and conditioning.

If you are willing to deepen your exploration of your unconsciousness, you will see that there is a lot more than just physiological and sensory processing that lies beyond your regular reach. You will discover that there are self-images (i.e., identities) buried within you. When I say identities, I really mean it, just like in movies that depict people with dissociative identity disorder (DID, a.k.a multiple personality disorder). However, in contrast with someone who really meets the criteria for DID, you and I fluidly transition between these personalities, usually gradually, and these personalities (also known in psychological jargon as "parts") know about each other. For example, if you examine yourself, you can notice that you act differently in various scenarios. There is the "you" that goes to work and conducts itself in the office. Then there is a personality that comes out with your spouse. There is another "you" with your best friend (when you can be yourself). There is the "you" with your parents. And then there is the you that plays sports, has sex, talks to the cashier, and goes to the beach. It is all the same person but different palettes of language tone, nonverbal features, and sometimes very specific behaviors (e.g., someone who only drinks socially).

Parts are developed to cope and adapt to life, to adapt and fit into the environment. Sometimes, these parts have reactions and behaviors that threaten the entire system. For example, say a five-year-old boy who got slapped in the face by another boy reacted by cowering in fear. In his family, his father was a Vietnam War vet, so fear was absolutely not tolerated. When the boy showed fear to his father, he immediately got scolded and was threatened with rejection. That part or identity is now forbidden, ashamed, and exiled out of consciousness into the dark shadow of the unconscious.

A teenage girl notices her female peers are developing their breasts, but hers are taking a bit longer. Some make fun of her flat torso. She feels embarrassed and ashamed and goes to her mother, who responds with, "Don't feel ashamed, sweetie. You don't have any reason to feel ashamed." But embarrassment and shame are a normal part of human psychology (although there is a problem if they become chronic and integrated into one's identity). Now, this girl's shame is exiled out of consciousness. It has no permission to be.

We all have many psychological parts that are repressed and unexpressed unless triggered or provoked. We all have shame, guilt, and monsters inside of us that can erupt in anger and sometimes bite our kids' heads off. We all have addictive and even violent parts. Most of them will never voice themselves, but we could hear the echoes of their voices in our lives if we only bothered to pay attention. I highly recommend experimenting with "parts" work in Internal Family Systems (IFS). Find a good therapist specializing in this modality and see for yourself.

Thoughts move from the unconscious into the conscious. How deep will you be willing to go to see them emerge? Can you also notice the forbidden ones? Those that tell you to stab someone, to crash your car into the concrete barrier, to steal a toothbrush at the store, or to touch someone in a forbidden way?

Lastly, as I experience reality, given my spiritual development, I can tell you that from my perspective, there is no objective world. We are always "inside." We are the mind, consciousness itself, and all that appears in it. The deeper you go into the unconscious, the more "things" will emerge that you will not be able to explain: archetypal images and identities, body sensations, energetic phenomena, entities, scenes from "past lives," and so on. For example, I was confronted with thousands and thousands of faces appearing in meditation, one after the other, for a couple of years before these were released from my mind. There is no separation between people and the divine, which can manifest in the mind in countless ways.

Resistance to Change

Resistance to change is a real force in our world. You can see it on a personal and systematic level (e.g., bureaucracy). People, in general, do not like change. They come into therapy or personal work settings and seek improvement in their symptoms, as they want to feel less depressed or anxious and happier. However, when true change is on the line and threatens the ego's status quo, clients begin to exhibit resistance to change processes in creative ways.

Jeff was freshly divorced in his early 60s. He was a very financially successful man who was now sitting in my office because of his sex, alcohol, and food addiction. He was scheduled for gastric bypass surgery a week from our session due to his obesity, a result of unhealthy life habits.

Jeff had a rich history of being abandoned by his father, neglected by his suicidal mother and becoming her caregiver, and bullied for years by peers in school. Yet, there was not a hint of anger on the surface, only the deep heaviness of depression. After engaging in some inner child work, he received a task to write a letter to his parents from a seven-year-old perspective and tell them about his feelings. Seems like a simple task, but it took him six months and two full-day MDMA journeys with a guide to be able to write it. Anger finally came out despite ego's best attempts to keep it at bay. Work had to be done to help Jeff realize that anger wouldn't be unconsciously incorporated into a new identity (i.e., "I'm an angry guy."). Interestingly, a day after his first MDMA journey, Jeff canceled his surgery and was able to get to a normal body weight within a year by following a simple diet and exercise regimen. All the energy of undigested emotional experiences was shed from his body naturally once he was willing to face them. This translated into an immediate shedding of physical weight.

There are a few common forms of resistance:

Forgetting—We tend to forget things that promote deep change in our ego machine. We forget to practice meditation, exercise, be kinder to ourselves and others, and practice skills we learned in sessions.

Falling asleep—I often see this in meditation and individuals reporting their medicine work. Clients will fall asleep when confronted with deeper truths about themselves that are too powerful to accept. This is very common when working with powerful entheogens such as 5-MeO-DMT. Many individuals experience "blacking out" or losing consciousness when taking this medicine.

Oppositional attitude—"I don't want to." Mostly seen in kids, teenagers, and immature adults (I'm sure you know some of those).

Difficulty going inside—Refusal or apparent inability to explore inner space or have any interaction with the unconscious.

Sylvia, an anxious mother in her 40s, was unable to close her eyes in response to hypnotic suggestions, guided meditations, or even medicine work with a guide. If she closed her eyes, she would open them within several seconds. In MDMA journeys, she would not let go of interpersonal interactions with the guide and would not stop talking. She could not breathe or feel her beingness or heart space. In psilocybin journeys, she would be assaulted with visions of insects and dragons (often these visions appear as archetypal symbols of guardians of the boundary between consciousness and the unconscious). In breathwork, she would just stop breathing within several seconds and not engage further in the process, often making complaints such as "I don't like the music" or reverting into interpersonal interaction: "You must think I'm stupid. What do you think about this style of music?"

Bret, a 30-year-old male, spent the first four months of his life in an incubator after multiple resuscitations, tubes coming in and out of his body and surrounded by the constant noise of machines, light, and medical personnel trying to keep him alive. He was also engulfed in the energy of a mother terrified for her premature boy's life and depressed, as the baby's biological father had abandoned them both. His fear of going into his unconscious and exploring repressed content was so severe that he would not stop moving in guided medicine journeys. This movement was a way to avoid what might be seen if he were still. However, after receiving the corrective experience he needed (e.g., of nurturing and feeling safe), he was able to let go of resistance and deepen his experience of the unconscious.

Resistance can be very frustrating for therapists and guides who are focused on a goal. Yet, if we allow people to determine for themselves how quickly they want to progress, resistance becomes the entrée of our time together. In essence, resistance to our true nature is the name of the game and should be attended to with care and compassion.

Common Presentations and Psychological Diagnoses

I've decided to talk about mental health disorders although I cannot stand this term. It is important to discuss these terms, which are commonly used in the healthcare, mental health care, and personal development arenas. More importantly, they are ego illnesses and, in some cases, the results of organic brain processes about which we understand very little in my humble opinion.

I personally almost never mention diagnoses to clients or even think about these when I work with someone. The less of a conceptual container I have in my mind about an individual, the freer and more accessibly the work flows through us as a vehicle of relationship and intimacy. More about that later.

As psychologists, we are trained to use the *Diagnostic and Statistical Manual of Mental Disorders* (DSM). It is written to provide physicians (i.e., psychiatrists) and mental health workers with a common vocabulary and conceptual constructs for working with a wide spectrum of psychological presentations. This is useful in research and also tailored to work with the healthcare insurance system, but that system is flawed to its very core. The flaw lies in the idea that an individual's health should be insured in case something goes *wrong*, versus an active "free for all" system that serves all members of society at all times and is funded by a dedicated, significant portion of a country's GDP.

While going to school, I spent many semesters memorizing the DSM in courses on psychopathology and psychological assessment, trying to learn by heart the symptoms of the unique presentation each mental health disorder has. It is a pathological approach that focuses on finding what is wrong with an individual. Although the pathological approach is insufficient, in my opinion, when conducting therapeutic work, having some background understanding of this domain is important.

There are two main issues I have with the pathological approach:

1. Although it might be beneficial initially for an individual to understand that their symptoms are part of a common phenomenon (e.g., depression, anxiety, PTSD, etc.), the diagnosis soon becomes integrated into the "story of me," and now, as a part of the ego, has a life of its own, defenses, and an agenda to preserve itself as a facet of identity.

2. The pathological approach creates a focus on a presentation of symptoms, which means the therapist-client relationship is aimed at reducing symptoms via direct or indirect approaches. This is a distraction from what the focus should be, which is self-*discovery* and shifting away from absolute ego-identification into partial ego-identification and, finally, into non-identification.

Remembering that, let's visit some of the common psychospiritual presentations and how they show up.

DEPRESSION

This is usually referred to as major depressive disorder (MDD) or dysthymia and is very common across all ages, ethnicities, and genders. In contrast to a bad mood, which usually lasts from several hours to a few days, depression is heavier, is devoid of energy, and encompasses all areas of life.

Most of the people I see with this condition have been helplessly beaten by life (e.g., by chronic illness or pain, major traumas, a stuck marriage, a complicated loss, a major change in life like retirement or a relationship shift, being a young mother to a kid on the spectrum, etc.) with no resolution in sight. Depression manifests in such conditions as a coping skill in which the bodymind decides to hibernate partially and lower the volume of much of experience. This often feels heavy and numb. Energy does not flow well to the legs or extremities. Usually, there is no feeling in the chest and heart chakra or a feeling of extreme heaviness that, with attention, usually evolves into pain. Over time, the individual wants to get back to life, but as the depression has settled, the bodymind is not easily convinced to return to the previous baseline, especially if depression has been integrated into the identity. Repeated failures to return to "ourselves" become painful and induce a great deal of suffering, which could result in suicidal ideation.

As an insider of the world of psychology, I can tell you that the success rates in treating MDD in the long term are not great. Most people will recover from it using antidepressants and psychotherapy, but relapse rates are relatively high, and many remain on antidepressants for many years. In addition, once they move out of depression, grief, or any other life-changing reality, most people remain fearful depression could grip them again.

Timothy is someone who comes to mind when I think about depression. In his late 50s and with a successful career in the high-tech industry, he was super dysthymic. Sundays were his worst days because he did not know what to do with himself if he did not have to work. Twenty years of antidepressants had very limited effect, and there were repeated issues with developing tolerance to these compounds. Those medications and CBT helped him remain alive, but he was still feeling lost and had no appetite for life.

In his case, Wim Hof breathwork, cold showers, and daily meditation were the beginning of an identity shift that allowed further development on his life journey. His depression was lifted in about two weeks of daily practice, and passion began to return to his life. Then, a microdose of psilocybin and an MDMA journey with a guide launched him on a completely new path in life. He was excited to know his inner world, which was also reflected in his awakened passion to devour life in the external world.

To summarize, in my opinion, and based on my experience, continual resistance and active refusal to release an undigested emotional experience eventually leads to depression, but there are pathways available to get out of it.

ANXIETY (GENERALIZED ANXIETY DISORDER AND OCD)

I find it amazing how many people walk around with anxiety and how much they underestimate its effects on their lives.

Dorothy, a mother of two children in her 40s, was paralyzed by anxiety for most of her adult life. Her anxiety was in her thoughts, imagining and ruminating on the worst possible scenarios: dying, getting sick, her children being hurt, financial hardships, and geopolitical events. It affected her body as rashes, chronic pain, and hormonal irregularities. Any new sensation in her body would immediately be categorized under the "Danger! Danger!" category: "What is wrong with this part of my body?"

Bob, on the other hand, was a retired physician who couldn't stop following certain mental routines that made him feel safe. He was obsessed with worrying about finances, although he never lacked any money. Every time worry about finances would come up (i.e., several times a day), he'd launch into mentally counting items or numbers. He wanted to stop worrying and counting in his head but couldn't bring himself to do so. In fact, he had been doing it in secret since the age of ten and was tormented by this behavior. This was further exacerbated by the shame and deep belief that something was inherently wrong with him.

Both Dorothy and Bob had very limited success with contemporary psychotherapy and psychotropic medications. Bob spent years on benzodiazepines, which eventually stopped working and had negative side effects on his life. He described the withdrawal from benzos as "the worst months of my life." Dorothy spent several years on SSRIs, but "They didn't change me; they were a Band-Aid that eventually stopped working even though I tried to switch them up several times."

Neither Dorothy nor Bob was able to engage in meditation or hypnosis in treatment. They were locked in their minds, with very little willingness or ability to dive deeper or access their bodies. The only thing that initiated a process of change was medicine work. The guide in both their cases was able to gradually progress with them. As the medicine opened their brains to change, they were able to integrate more practices into their lives and become more intimate with themselves and their bodies.

Dorothy still has anxiety but is now engaged in life. She flies, fights with her ex-husband (versus cowering in fear and submitting to his ridiculous attitude), and is attentive to her body. Bob no longer meets the criteria for OCD. They both have a long journey ahead of them, but there is a feeling of flow in their lives.

PTSD AND COMPLEX TRAUMA

War, rape, sexual abuse, molestation, car accidents, traumatic illnesses, surgeries, cancer, miscarriage, witnessing a death or crime, taking your infant son into the ocean out of stupidity and almost losing him in the waves. Events that you cannot forget. The emotions embedded in these memories are so deep and full of fear that, despite your best attempts, biology takes over.

I was taken completely off-guard when my first therapist told me I had a complex form of PTSD. Lisa took me on for my PhD program's required psychotherapy hours. I was surprised and unsurprisingly resistant, as I did not meet the DSM criteria. However, I was moving about my day with an underlying dread that something bad was waiting just around the corner. I only had to let my guard down for a minute, and I knew that life was again going to bite me right on the butt.

It took me a while to see it, but eventually, all the pieces fell into place. I had a case of complex trauma resulting from growing up in a dysfunctional family where, at any moment, liquidators could walk in and take any possessions we had. Where every day my parents' health and life were questionable. It was enough to leave a residue of undigested fear, a samskara that wanted to be liberated via experience. And experiencing it was the farthest thing from my mind for many years.

Axel is another good example. He was a good-looking active-duty special forces soldier who walked smoothly into my office. The only reason he was sitting on my couch was because he was fighting a six-month-long battle with a persistent urge to kill himself. Then the trembling and shaking started, panic attacks that would not let go. His body was betraying him despite all the training and the steel focus of his mind. It is hard to place explosives and shoot people in the head when your hands shake uncontrollably.

He would have killed himself, but he had a son and wife he deeply loved and cared for. He absolutely could not go to the Navy for help. He would be taken off active duty instantly, he would abandon his team, and there would be complications. His career would be over if anyone were to find out. So, he came to me, under the table; his real name was never written anywhere, and no one will ever know.

I see many others like him: military personnel, federal agents, police officers, teachers, social workers, judges. If you are a part of the system, you must be perfect. At the very least, you must pretend that you do not smoke weed, take antidepressants, get stressed out, or have a biological machine operating within you with significant needs.

Back to Axel. As I started inquiring into his body perception, he became very stiff. It was an easy clue to understanding that his focus was so powerful that he was able to surpass a great deal of his severe PTSD symptoms beneath the blanket of consciousness. But it was taking a toll on his body, and the nerves were releasing steam as best they could.

In trauma, the samskaras and undigested emotional content are powerful. These create massive pressure on the energy body and our physiological nervous system. Samskaras want to liberate and release themselves. With PTSD, we usually speak of fear. *The* fear. An absolute total terror. The amygdala (a nucleus of the brain's limbic system, a.k.a. the brain's alarm bell) fires repeatedly and eventually locks up. Then you're stuck in loops of panic attacks, fear of panic attacks, or just unbearable dread. It does not matter how strong you are or what kind of willpower you have. Repeated and chronic exposure to frightening events will eventually take a toll on your biology. Then the brain circuitry will be imprinted to follow a certain pathway in which fear is the core of our existence.

In Axel's case, the samskara was attempting to release itself. Energy wanted to return to the source. To heal this requires you to be willing to have a conscious experience of the pain, fear, or somatic sensation, sometimes even without understanding what you are experiencing. I am glad to say that Axel was able to give birth to that experience and move on with his life.

DISSOCIATION

I would like to dedicate a few words to discussing dissociation. In the DSM, dissociation appears as a separate chapter, which discusses DID, depersonalization, and derealization. However, in the field, symptoms of dissociation usually manifest in connection with trauma. Often, the person feels as if they are not in their body. There is numbness, a feeling that the world is unreal, or general detachment from emotions, oneself, and others. Dissociation is normally considered a negative state of being. However, if considered from the view described in this book, it is actually a matter of perspective.

What happens is that, following a traumatic event, the ego becomes fragmented or, in some cases, disintegrates completely for some time. As that happens, there is a spontaneous revelation of our true nature, our naked consciousness. Our regular identity and the way we connect to the world break down. This is a glimpse of our true nature that can be a wonderful opportunity for spiritual expansion and a shift to a more whole and inclusive identity.

However, for individuals who do not understand what is happening to them, there is an attempt to go back to the ego, to the way things were before the accident, rape, cancer, battle, and so on. This is even more severe if the trauma happened at an early age, before the ego had a chance to form cohesively, and the person is attempting to construct an ego, although they unconsciously already know, due to the glimpse into consciousness, that there is something deeper and more expansive than the ego.

Dissociation can be very unpleasant. In some cases, the suffering it induces is so severe that it leads to depression, substance abuse, and sometimes suicide attempts. It is important to assess if the individual is ready to change their focus, let go of the attachment to the ego, and find themselves in a new identity that is spiritually bound. If not, we can still help them to find grounded presence in their body and psyche. In IFS terminology, this means that identity has to shift from the ego and parts into the Self.

AUTISM SPECTRUM AND ATTENTION-DEFICIT/
HYPERACTIVITY DISORDER (ADHD)

Andrew, a 26-year-old bear of a man, was afflicted with being easily overwhelmed by his senses (especially sound and touch) and emotional outbursts. I spent more than ten years evaluating individuals with autism and other developmental conditions. The best that the world of psychiatry and psychology currently has to offer is behavioral and medical management, social skills training, and familial support. These interventions have made a significant improvement for Andrew and many others. However, the true change that would allow him to look into people's eyes without a stress response in his body and decrease his emotional reactivity was always out of reach.

If you search PubMed, you will find some very interesting studies about the use of LSD and psilocybin with individuals, including children, who were suffering from schizophrenia and autism in the '50s and '60s. Unfortunately, all these studies were discontinued following the move to categorize most psychedelic substances as illegal under the Controlled Substances Act of 1970.

Andrew actually went very far diving deeper into his being with meditation, hypnosis, and parts work (i.e., IFS). His emotional dysregulation had subsided. He no longer thought of himself as a monster, and many of his core beliefs about himself and the world had changed. He was more flexible with himself and the world than he ever had been. However, some of the neurological presentations often seen among people on the spectrum or with ADHD were still present. It was not until he started working with psilocybin in guided sessions that he could begin to see real changes in his body and his nervous system. He was finally able to open up to a group of people and make eye contact, and his brain seemed to be better able to digest sensory inputs that had previously overwhelmed him.

I would like to say a few words about ADHD. In summary, I see it as a "basket diagnosis" that is often too easily given to people in order to justify the administration of cognitive enhancers such as Ritalin, Concerta, and their cousins. Do not get me wrong, some people really do have neurological presentations that cause significant difficulties in sustaining attention and being hyperactive, and sometimes using cognitive enhancers makes sense. But when you see the range of presentations in hospitals and county-level settings, it is not hard to notice that most people who are diagnosed with ADHD are actually suffering from anxiety, a significant lack of self-confidence, or an acute addiction to electronics in a dopamine-dependence cycle (similar to cocaine). Procrastination, in my experience, is about anxiety, not ADHD.

If you think you have ADHD, please seek an evaluation from a psychologist rather than from your family doctor, who will prescribe amphetamines to see if they will benefit you or not. Moreover, even if you do suffer from ADHD, like autism, it is not a condition that needs to be managed only behaviorally or medically. You can actually make significant improvements to your life using meditation and deep work.

PSYCHOSIS AND SPIRITUAL EMERGENCIES

Sam, a 17-year-old, gentle, and sweet young man, was brought to my office by his parents, who are both very educated and successful and had high expectations for their son. He had started smoking weed a few weeks before with his buddies, and his life took an expected turn when light bulbs started talking to him. He began hearing discorporate whispers. It was not yet a full-blown psychotic episode, but things were getting weirder by the day. This was also a very common age for the onset of schizophrenia, which often begins with a stressful life event or following the use of psychoactive substances. His parents were genuinely concerned.

Sam's parents thought about the psychiatric route but had both had family members who were psychiatrically hospitalized for many years and did not want to go down that path. I have worked in psychiatric inpatient units and have very close professional relationships with several psychiatrists. I knew what was going to be in store for Sam if we went through the regular path of antipsychotics and inpatient hospitalization. As Sam was not a danger to himself or others, we decided together to address his symptoms differently.

When we moved deeper via hypnotherapy and sensation of his body, we discovered that Sam was a very spiritual person and that he was struggling with deep existential questions. In addition, we also quickly discovered that a lot of energy was moving in his body and that he was actually experiencing an initial awakening in the form of kundalini energy movement that was affecting his brain and cognitive processes. Within several weeks of meditation, physical exercises, and abstinence from marijuana, his "psychosis" faded, and he returned to a stable and normal state of consciousness. In addition, he was now much more aware of his inner world and energy body. Currently, Sam is about to graduate college and living a stable life.

Working with the Ego

Our work with the ego depends on where we want to go. Many clients I work with have no interest in discovering their true nature. Their passion for spirituality is still not yet awakened.

In the following pages, I will share examples of deep work with people and the venues that enable those levels of work.

However, I want to emphasize one very important point. The goal at any level of personal development is not to eradicate the ego or our personality in any way whatsoever. The goal is to have a somatic and perceptual shift from being completely identified with the ego and its associated physical body to an identity in which the ego is but a part of who we are. Then we become more identified with our true nature, which includes the ego. In doing so, we actually experience more freedom to be ourselves as a unique expression of nature. Our ego almost receives a blessing to be itself, with its imperfections, in what now appears to be a perfect dynamic play.

I always thought that after awakening, I would change for the better. That I would stop smoking weed or be a better father. But what I can say is that my relationship with my ego got lighter and easier. My body moves the same, thoughts come and go, and I still do stupid things sometimes. What changed is the rigidity that I had about being a "certain person," the control that I attempted to exert over my inner and outer reality, and the introduction of a tremendous sense of calm that the world is perfect as it is.

Here are some examples to show the various depths of work that are achievable with different individuals with different capacities and settings. The sky is the limit to how much change can happen in someone's life, given their motivation and courage.

Level 1: Behavioral Changes

At this level, the change is predominantly behavioral. It is possible via coaching or a discussion with a friend or family member who has a strong personality and a systematic, logical approach to life.

A client walks into my office and is upset because his credit score went down from 900 to 620 because he forgot to make several consecutive payments on an almost unused credit card. The client is pissed that, although he has been "behaving flawlessly" financially over the last decade, two months of careless mistakes caused such an extreme repercussion. I also often see this with people who receive a DUI. The client's anger at this point is directed at the world that "harmed" them. It is unfair, and although they had some responsibility for it, in their opinion, the system should have worked better. Furthermore, an attempt to shine light on the client's part in this issue is often met with resistance and anger.

Usually, such a client will need some ego bandaging and positive experiences to improve their self-image. Then, building a structured behavioral plan will "ensure" financial stability, gradually increasing the credit score, and reaffirm in the client's mind that this will never happen again.

Level 2: Cognitive Changes

From the credit card company's perspective, two missing payments are indicative of a current change in the client's attitude. Something significant has changed in the client's life, since he has been paying consistently for years, either an external or an internal event. From its perspective, the company can say that, at least temporarily, the client's risk level has increased. Something is happening to him, and we should pay attention to him, so his credit score goes down.

Explaining this to the client via psychoeducation or another simple intervention is a form of *reframing*. Now the client has more context about this event, which will decrease his emotional reactivity, as "this is not personally about me." This is usually done in CBT or by an intuitive, empathetic friend. This level of work targets cognitive distortions and deflects emotion and negative thoughts. The client can better rationalize the situation, decrease catastrophizing, and promote an attitude of willingness to face current reality.

Level 3: Deeper Cognition and Exploration of Beliefs

Directly facing the client's behavior—"How come you missed the payment?"—is more common in psychodynamic therapy.

This is usually met with resistance and often a mental chess game has to be played: "What is going on with you? Forget about the credit card company, how come after ten years you are not paying attention?"

Client: "It's not my fault. The card I was using to pay that card expired."

Therapist: "Have you had cards expire before?"

Client pretends to think: "Yes."

Therapist: "How many times?"

Client: "Several times."

Therapist: "How come you always noticed it before?"

Client: "I'm good at managing our finances."

Good, we're getting somewhere.

Therapist: "That's interesting, right? I also have the same impression. It doesn't fit you." (Zooming out a bit to get some perspective and enable him to dissociate from his identity to give deeper feedback about his *story*.)

Client: "I know, something is wrong with me. Do you think I'm depressed?"

Great. Now we have something to work with, and we have shifted attention from "What's wrong with the world?" to "I need to take a good look at myself."

Level 4: Emotions

This stage is about moving into the body.

Therapist: "When you think about your credit score dropping, what do you feel?"

Client: "I'm furious. How dare they?!"

Therapist: "You're angry!"

Client: "Yeah!"

Therapist: "What does it feel like in your body to experience this?"

Client: "I hate it. I hate feeling angry. I hate it that they made me feel that."

Therapist: "Where do you sense this?"

Client: "My hands are tight, and I just want to smash something. My face feels hot."

Therapist: "I understand your anger. But I'd like to examine it more deeply. Is that okay?"

Client: "Okay . . . "

Therapist: "Let's close our eyes . . . Take a deep breath . . . Now focus on the sensation in your chest. Give it attention even though it's counterintuitive. What does it feel like?"

Client: "It feels cold and tight. I don't like it."

Therapist: "I know. It doesn't feel good. You don't have to like it but try for a minute to make more space for it. Almost say 'I allow this feeling to be there.'"

Client: "I don't want to do that."

Therapist: "And what does that feel like?"

Client: "It feels stuck. It makes me even more angry."

Therapist: "How long have you been feeling this stuck feeling?"

Client: "Since I can remember."

Therapist: "It's not fun, right? So, let's try something else, just for a few minutes."

Client: "Okay."

Therapist: "Give the feeling space. Allow it."

Client: "I allow it."

Therapist: "Now watch it."

. . .

Client: "It changes. It feels lighter."

The client's face begins to change. There is distress on his face, an attempt to prevent something from rising to the surface.

Therapist: "What is happening now?"

Client: "I'm scared."

Now we are getting to something deeper that was triggered recently and, in a cascading chain of events, caused the client's recent forgetfulness in paying his bills. For example, here's a plausible scenario with different variations that I have seen: The client's spouse becomes busier at work. This causes the client to feel that the relationship is threatened. He worries that she will become disinterested in him. Fear is triggered. However, fear is forbidden for him as a man and with his specific psychology. Nevertheless, the energy of the emotion (i.e., a samskara) is present in his body and wants to be released. The client self-sabotages by "forgetting" to pay the credit card bill. This brings consequences that result in anger. He is now able to shift his fear into anger, direct it at an external party, and deflect that fear.

Level 5: MDMA (Psychedelic Medicine) Session

This level of work grants access to deeper layers and also a clearer examination on the client's part. Many individuals who work with MDMA describe the clarity and owl-like vision of the experience that help them see into the dynamics of their inner and outer life. Anxiety and psychological resistance are largely, if not entirely, removed on the client side by the medicine. In addition, the heart opening usually associated with MDMA increases feelings of compassion for oneself and others.

This level of work is also possible in trance work, parts work, or any work that attempts to penetrate deeper. However, MDMA, when used correctly with an experienced guide and the right set and setting, accelerates the process dramatically from weeks, months, and years into a single session. It also significantly increases the intimacy and psychological safety in the relationship between therapist and client. These are all important factors in the therapeutic process. The client is able to project onto the therapist various psychological parts that can be both benevolent and malicious, which aids in processing forbidden inner parts. A skilled therapist can utilize this in various ways to expose psychological parts and processes and address them compassionately.

For example, during an MDMA session, the client is able to connect to his fear through sensations in the body.

Client: "I feel my heart center again. It's tight. It's the fear."

Therapist: "Go deeper into the fear. I am here with you. You are safe. Allow it to manifest if you can. What is it like?"

Client: "I see my mom. She left. I see the day she left."

The client begins to talk extensively (very common in MDMA sessions) and feel the betrayal he experienced as a child when his mother left the house, escaping his drunk father who had lost control of his life. The client is able to feel the fear of losing his mother and staying behind with his unstable father, as well as the anger over his mother's betrayal. Once he is able to connect to these experiences and emotions as an adult and empathetically love the child inside of him who went through all of that, the heart center opens completely.

Such an opening often translates immediately into a life-changing force. The client is very likely to become more relaxed, more empathetic, and better connected to his emotions and body and have more available psychic energy that was previously dedicated to the effort to keep unprocessed experiences and emotions underneath the surface of consciousness. Such effort often translates into increased baseline stress in the nervous system and the various tissues of the body, usually concluding in various somatic symptoms that release excess stress, such as acne, rashes, asthma, allergies, bloating and digestive disorders, inflammation, arthritis, anxiety and panic attacks, depression, and, in some cases, tics and other peripheral nervous symptoms.

In some cases, such a heart opening can last days or weeks, often igniting a spiritual spark, spiritual in the sense that the client will understand that there are many layers to their being they were previously unaware of.

The client can also understand that, despite their ignorance, these layers directly affect their life on a daily basis. They will become interested in diving deeper only to discover that the rabbit hole goes very, very deep, way beyond their imagination.

Level 6: Psilocybin and Deep Spiritual States

The previous level is also achievable when working with psilocybin mushrooms. However, as fungi are living beings, when consumed, the "spirit" of the mushroom has an agenda and is, therefore, much more unpredictable. MDMA usually turns ego defenses off and allows one to examine their reality from the higher-self perspective. With mushrooms, the work begins with our self, our defenses, samskaras, and our energy body, and also with other realities, other dimensions of beings, experiences of unity consciousness, being able to experience life from perspectives of other beings (e.g., cows, flowers, butterflies, etc.), and, finally, the experience of a temporary ego dissolution that further clarifies one's true nature and identity.

It is important to note that this level of work is absolutely achievable via meditation and other profound spiritual and mystical experiences. It can also happen spontaneously, but that is quite rare or requires consistent practice and effort. The experience of a temporary ego dissolution facilitates the discovery of the "Self" as a primary baseline identity that lies beyond our personality, body image, and personal history. This can be a visceral and ultimate understanding that the ego is a process rather than a fixed identity. The benefit of this is ultimately a complete and total liberation and, for most people, an initiation into a process that will flower over the span of a lifetime.

Level 7: Integration, "I Got It. I Lost It."

Despite the discovery of the Self, life continues. Perhaps you have noticed that even famous awakened individuals who went through profound mystical experiences still experience anger, grief, sadness, attachment, addictive behaviors, sickness, and death. What changes is the identification with ego identity and a gradual transition into identification with our true nature. Such an identification also carries a pleasant side effect of an increase in freedom to live life and experience inner and outer reality as it is. However, for most people, this transition in identification is gradual and often consists of the experience "I got it! I lost it!" Patterns of identification, self-images, and samskaras resurface and seem to have a life of their own.

This is caused by what is referred to in Eastern philosophies as karmic traces. In Western psychology and Jungian psychology, it is often referred to as the shadow. These are aspects of individual and collective unconscious material that, unless resolved and unburdened or purified, will come back again and again in an attempt to release themselves.

The work in psychedelic-assisted psychotherapy, especially with psilocybin mushrooms, is potent in revealing unconscious shadows and karmic traces. Such work is also possible using hypnosis and parts work (IFS) but is usually more rapid under the influence of psychedelic substances when conducted in an appropriate set and setting.

Nevertheless, one of the dangers in such work is overfixating on the shadow and internal phenomena rather than focusing on becoming grounded and certain of one's true nature. More specifically, prior to the recognition that we have an inner world, clients are fixated on the experience of external phenomena. There is a compulsive obsession with changing and engaging with the external world via entertainment (e.g., videos and video games), a career, love, relationships, food, and so on. Once the internal world opens up more fully, the recognition of thoughts, feelings, sensations in the body, energetic phenomena, visions, and mystical rapture brings about more varied phenomena that clients could potentially fixate on, distracting them from progression on the path of seeking the ultimate truth about one's being.

For example, in one of the most powerful psilocybin journeys I have ever had, I saw myself standing with a bloody axe over the bodies of women and children in a narrow canyon. I knew that I had butchered them and was faced with my darker side. I was captivated, dove into my shadow, and found myself spending a year trying to understand. Because the narrative was so powerful and disturbing, I became addicted to figuring it out and was entertained by the need to put things in place conceptually. By the end of it, I found that I had forgotten the path of self-recognition.

The hallmark of this level is the experience of "I got it! I lost it!" which is common in spiritual schools such as Dzogchen, Mahamudra, and non-dual Shaivism. You have discovered a unity state where your ego disappears for periods of time, but eventually, the ego comes back. It has the force of a habit.

Self-delusion, forgetting who we truly are, is one of the most powerful forces in creation. The ego survives. It functions and justifies its existence by appropriating every experience, including spiritual ones: "I (the little me) have realized it!" All experiences eventually become "my" experience. When a client enters shadow work, the self-narrative gets amplified. People get very interested in their shadow, and most will spend years and decades digging, healing, and conceptually trying to understand that which ultimately cannot be understood, as the truth lies beyond the capacities of the conceptual mind.

In order to keep most individuals from driving themselves into pitfalls, many spiritual traditions forbid or discourage followers from using substances to progress on the spiritual path, as the risk of being trapped by the power and content of the psychedelic experience is substantial and real.

However, in the 21st century, given the risks that humanity is facing, it is irresponsible, in my humble opinion, to ignore the varied benefits that psychedelic substances can offer in quickening human, emotional, social, and spiritual development. I had similar concerns in the past, which I expressed to my root teacher. She replied by asking me, "Have you tried brushing your teeth without toothpaste? Why not use something that nature has provided us? A fruit of the gods."

I think that the use of psychedelics in this work is appropriate, especially for clients who are interested in spiritual development, understanding the "True Self," and connecting with the divine or facing end-of-life junctions. However, if psychedelics are to be used, then spiritual orientation, especially aimed at grounding oneself in awareness of awareness, is crucial for this stage.

Experiencing our shadow from a grounded perspective of self-recognition allows a deep dive into a total experience that is not focused on conceptual understanding. The aim is to liberate the narrative, let go of beliefs and judgments, and simply immerse in the consciousness in which emotional and energetic movements echo.

CHAPTER 4

THE PSYCHIC BODY

THERE ARE MANY DIFFERENT PERSPECTIVES ON AND REFERENCES TO OUR metaphysical bodies: the psychic body, the energy body, the subtle body, the emotional body, and so on. Some of these are synonymous. One way to visualize this is to imagine a human being as composed of many layers, like an onion. Some of these layers comprise the physical reality that we can see, touch, and measure using instruments (e.g., height, texture, weight, and electrical charge). Some are invisible and can't be measured with today's technology. These layers are not separated but are rather a spectrum of dimensions in fluid interaction and relationship with each other.

There are many theoretical systems that describe these layers, and I encourage you to study them if this is an area of interest to you. However, at this stage, in order to simplify the discussion and avoid confusion, I will be using the term "psychic body" and group most of the layers under this term.

Psychic and Inner Bodies

The psychic body is a metaphysical, energetic system that cannot be measured or observed. However, it can be felt and sensed. This body has the gross shape of our physical body and includes chakras, meridians, and a storage system of our entire history, including all other "lives."

If the physical body is the physical car we are driving, the psychic body is the gas, air, electricity, and software that runs our car. The psychic body has a lot of dents (i.e., samskaras) that constrict the flow of energy (i.e., prana, tsal). The psychic body also carries karma, the deep conditioning of our being to experience life in a certain way.

There is a tight relationship between the psychic and physical bodies.

In essence, the psychic body continually radiates the physical body. It energizes and, through such processes as cell generation, recreates the fabric of matter in every moment of existence. The radiation and creation of our physical body follow a unique blueprint that exists in the psychic body. The physical expression of this blueprint is DNA. The change in personality and physiological healing that people often seek requires changes on the level of the psychic body, that is, the release of samskaras and opening of chakras and energy channels (i.e., meridians).

Introduction to the Psychic Body

I met Shanti when, like many of my clients, she was at the end of her rope. A radiologist of East Indian descent, divorced, and mother to three children, she was in her early 40s, actively suicidal, and could not stop drinking. Her life had fallen apart around her during a recent affair with a married man. She did not know why she was drinking or what the problem was. Within a few minutes, I got the strong odor of a borderline personality disorder. If you know anything about therapists, it's that most of them will gently but firmly let such individuals exit their office and hope to never see them again ("I'm not the right person for you. I don't work with personality disorders. We're not a good match.").

In Shanti's case, however, chances were that, if I turned her away, a decline and suicide attempts would follow. SSRIs were not working anymore, and other medications would zonk her out beyond her ability to work and care for her children appropriately. Worst of all, she could not trust herself around men anymore and was left with almost no friendships. Although I was anxious about entering into an intimate relationship with her due to her personality disorder, as a father, I cared deeply about her children and the effects that her decline would have on their lives.

In meditative exercises, Shanti noticed that she could not feel much from the neck down. Her medically trained mind attempted to explain and categorize this, but I advised her to let her strong mind rest for a while. We went deeper with various somatic exercises. What came out was not a surprise for me or her. She always knew that she hated her father.

She suspected why but could not specifically remember what happened. As she dove deeper into her body, more content appeared in her consciousness.

I do not know what Shanti's father and other men did to her in early childhood and later in life. However, at the very least, I can say that the way she perceived what happened to her was severe sexual and physical abuse. Visions and images of abuse started surfacing in our time together, she had many nightmares, and classic PTSD symptoms began to emerge when she stopped drinking and taking SSRIs. In guided medicine journeys, despite her guide's attempts to be as gentle as possible in her process, energetic phenomena began to rapidly release from her body. The samskaras came out in intense ways: shakes, vivid memories, deep fear, and the return of sensations in the body, such as aches and pains. She started bleeding from her vagina in a session as memories of sexual abuse constellated.

The more permission Shanti's body received to release what was buried deep, the lighter she felt following the sessions. After about a year of deep work, she no longer drank, her PTSD symptoms vanished completely, and her relationships with others stabilized. She was no longer borderline (which is usually unheard of in the field of psychology). She was now in a solid relationship with a type of man who "I could never be with before; he just loves me. I always went after the bad guys."

As I move to describe the psychic body, I want to highlight that the following description is based on several systems but should not be considered definitive. In my understanding, there is no correct and objective way to describe any facet of reality. Scaffolding is not the building itself nor can it accurately describe the building underneath. Yet we cannot build or paint a building without proper scaffolding. It is a necessary part of the project. Similarly, the following exposition is scaffolding that can allow us to connect to facets of ourselves that are often hidden from individuals without proper training.

The common, contemporary view of the psychic or energy body (at least in American and European cultures) includes categorizing chakras and energy channels into corresponding emotional states and qualities. This is a conceptual imposition that arose from a misunderstanding of the original purpose and description of the chakra systems by key figures in the Theosophical movement. While I do not want to take away the gains people have had from working with the psychic body via impositions of emotions, I find it restrictive in the long term.

In summary, at times, it can be beneficial to associate chakras and energy with specific emotions. But I advise you not to become overly rigid with this approach and to invite an attitude of curiosity and exploration with energetic phenomena rather than attempting to read energy based on a preconceived conceptual map that you may have. As you dive deeper into the more subtle dimensions of reality (i.e., facets of reality that we normally do not experience), you will begin to experience energy movement in your body, and your understanding of it will become clearer. Your energetic expression and understanding are unique to you. Please do not try to generalize it to others. It can be confusing, as people have very different experiences around energetic phenomena in their bodies.

Now, with all of that in mind, I will share with you my understanding of the energy body so that the description might be a bridgehead for you to embark on your own journey. I will first describe the elements of a being (the onion layers) from subtle to gross.

SINGULARITY AND STILLNESS

The most subtle level, at the center of the onion, and even beyond the subtle level, is the realm of absolute nondual consciousness.

The core of a being is a point of singularity of absolute stillness. This is often referred to as Shiva in nondual Shaiva tantra or the Supreme Source, Samantabhadra, or dharmakaya in Dzogchen. Most people are never consciously aware of it, although it is always present with us in waking, dreaming, and sleeping. Everything manifests in and out of this point of stillness. This point of singularity can never be tainted, harmed, or modified in any way. It is beyond existence and nonexistence. It is not really a point but immense and infinite space. It does not exist spatially. There is, in fact, very little we can say about it. The only way to know it is by experiencing it and ultimately realizing that this deep stillness is what we are.

ENERGY

We know from modern astrophysics that the universe is expanding, and its rate of expansion is increasing. One way to think about energy is as the force that keeps pushing the universe and stretching it. From this perspective, energy is constantly pouring into the universe from the ground of being, the singularity. This energy is different than what we usually think of as electricity or thermodynamic energy. The energy I am talking about is alive and intelligent, not so much an entity sitting in another dimension and making plans as an organic process that has intuitive capacities. There are patterns to this energy, which is constantly radiating and manifesting reality.

It might be easier to call this energy "Shakti," which is the traditional name in nondual Shaiva tantra, to help us remember that it is alive and not just an inanimate force. Traditionally, Shakti is also worshipped as a goddess and has multiple divine manifestations (i.e., various goddess forms) that people can connect to devotionally (e.g., the divine mother, Parashakti, Kali, and so on.)

With respect to our bodies, there are several theories (such as Shakti in nondual Shaiva tantra, and sambhogakaya in Dzogchen) that describe the process by which energy creates the psychic body, the chakras, and meridians. If you have ever seen a corpse or someone shortly after they have passed, it is very noticeable that something is now "gone." What is missing is the flow of energy, which is the breath of life and what animates us from within. As energy pours into us, it builds our body, animates us, and creates thoughts, feelings, and perceptions. Energy enters and leaves. As it constitutes us, it also has the instinct to recycle back to the source. However, when we are unable to experience certain states, the energy gets stuck and, over time, crystallizes into a samskara.

BIOFIELD (AURA)

In prayer circles and the shamanic tradition, the term aura is commonly used. Auras have colors, dents, intensity, texture, and so on. Guides and energy workers who are more grounded in the scientific perspective use the term "biofield." A biofield is supposedly "an energy field that surrounds and permeates living organisms. It is believed to be a subtle electromagnetic or vibrational field that is not currently detectable by modern scientific instruments" (Foundation for Alternative and Integrative Medicine, 2021).

I cannot present any measurable data that can indicate whether the biofield or aura exists or not. However, from personal experience, I can easily say that when a person walks into a room, there is a feeling about them. They can be heavy, light, attractive, boring, disappearing into the background, and so on. When someone enters your personal space, you can feel them if you just pay attention, almost like magnets pushing too close to one another. I choose to call it a biofield. This is just a personal choice—whatever works.

My engagement with the biofield of another person is mostly informative in nature. I do not see auras but rather rely on a sense that is approximately a synthesis between touch and feeling. Synesthesia is a condition usually associated with psychedelic states of super-plasticity, but in fact, it can be learned after you have tasted it.

When I sit with people, I can "feel" my degree of comfort. Do I feel inclined to touch them or not? Is there anxiety in my body? Is there tension or a sensation of relaxation? Am I attracted to them emotionally, sexually, or physically? I understand that my mind projects on the feeling I have, but there is an original trigger that I've learned to see. It gives me a deeper understanding of someone's state in multiple domains.

I see the biofield of another person as a dynamic field of communication that we can learn to read. It almost has an identity and agenda of its own. It can "talk" to a skilled therapist via muscle testing and other methods. I know, it's weird. It's science fiction, but if it works, it works. Who am I to argue?

It takes skill to separate perceptions from labels and cognition, but it can be done. It is a mastery that only comes with practice.

The other way I interact with a biofield is during touch work, when I will consider the biofield of the client. How close do I sit? How intense is the touch? What are the changes in my body sensation as I provide touch?

I also ask permission from my client verbally and nonverbally to approach and make contact. I give some time for the client's biofield to get used to me and establish trust.

THE CENTRAL CHANNEL (I.E., SUSHUMNA) AND THE THREE BINDUS

As Shakti builds our body, the first thing that appears out of the point of singularity is what we call the central channel (i.e., the sushumna nadi). This channel is made of light, but not the kind of light you can see. You cannot touch or see the central channel, but you can feel it with practice. The central channel cannot be harmed, changed, or tainted in any way. It is essential to a being as the point of singularity. The central channel does not sit in the body. It is not in the spine. It lies in a different dimension that cannot be affected by physical reality. Although the central channel can never be tainted, our access to it (i.e., knowing, sensing, and directing our attention to it) can be blocked or decreased significantly because of energetic and psychological defenses.

In addition to the sushumna, there are also three powerful energetic centers called the three Bindus (in nondual Shaiva tantra) or the three dantians (in Taoism). These three spots, usually located in the head, heart, and lower belly, are considered to also be untainted and beyond the dimensions of physical reality. They are central to energetic and spiritual practice in all these traditions.

CONNECTING WITH THE PSYCHIC BODY

Out of the sushumna, energy radiates and creates the primary chakras, the meridians, and the body's energy field (i.e., the aura or biofield). These elements compose what I refer to as the psychic body. The chakras, meridians, and biofield are elements of being that can be affected by life experiences, emotions, beliefs, and so on.

The psychic body is the "place" where samskaras and karma are stored and manifest. More specifically, meridians get blocked or inflamed with stuck energy. Chakras can be "closed," not rotating, or collapsed on themselves and the biofield can be "colored" or accumulate "holes" or "walls." Furthermore, the psychic body holds the blueprint of our physical body. It directs the energy to build our cells on a daily basis, according to the patterns of flow. For example, the energy of anxiety and worry creates patterns in the nervous system, releasing certain hormones and neurotransmitters, affecting cells and our facial expressions. One way to think about the transition from energy into matter is the crystallization of energy. As energy accumulates in a location, it crystallizes and eventually manifests as matter.

If you have a musical mind, you can visualize a guitar and a certain chord. Let's say E major. There are 20 positions that could play the chord E but in different keys or octaves. In the same way, the physical body is the most basic position of the E major chord, and the psychic body is the same chord but in a higher key position. They both vibrate the same content but in different frequencies. The simplest way I can describe it is to imagine listening to Leonard Cohen singing "Hallelujah" (deep voice, low vibration—physical body) versus "Hallelujah" sung by Pavarotti (high voice, higher vibration—psychic body). Neither is more important than the other; both are needed for this specific performance.

The psychic body can be easily felt in yourself and others with a little bit of practice. For example, think about the presentation of three different individuals walking into a room in the midst of a dinner party. The first has an irresistible charisma. We can say that their aura is open and inviting. The second individual has a very heavy energy field, which often indicates depression. The third has a prickly feel. Do not trigger or touch them in any way whatsoever, as they might explode.

There are many meditations and spiritual practices that are aimed at connecting, exploring sensing, and, eventually, spontaneously identifying with stillness, the central channel, and, lastly, with movement, However, this section focuses on work with the psychic body, since that is where most people get stuck, as obstacles, samskaras, and other energetic phenomena prevent or slow down spiritual and personal development. In addition, the psychic body plays an integral part in our day-to-day existence, and learning how to work with it can greatly improve one's life.

Chakras

The word "chakra" (in Sanskrit: *cakra*) literally means wheel or circle. When we talk about chakras, we refer to centers of energy in our psychic body where there is a junction of many meridians (channels) coming together or where there is a perceived center of activity or sensation.

The most common Euro-American view on chakras in the seven-chakra system is depicted in illustration 1. At times, chakras will be given specific colors and associated emotions, depending on the tradition.

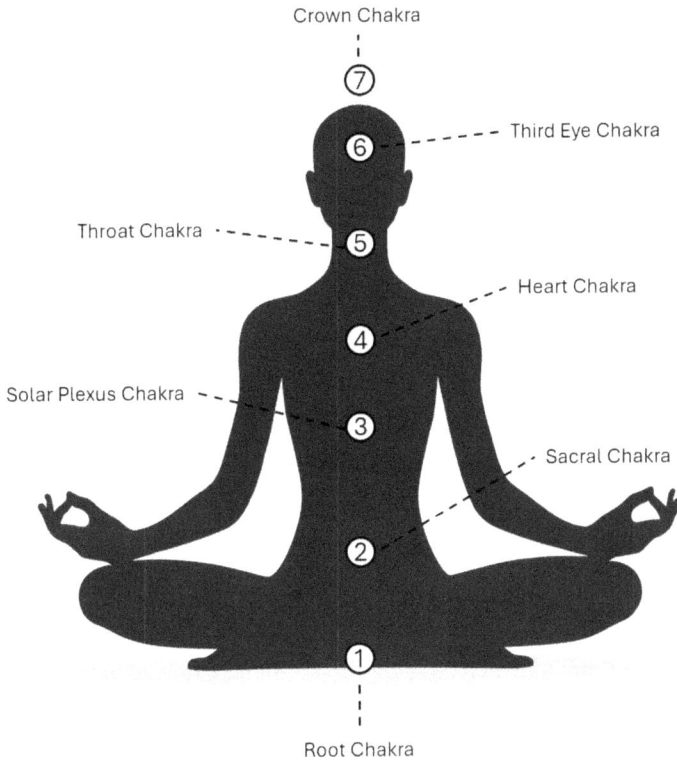

Crown Chakra

⑦

⑥ - - - - - Third Eye Chakra

Throat Chakra · - - - - - ⑤

- - Heart Chakra

④

Solar Plexus Chakra - - - - - ③

- · Sacral Chakra

②

①

Root Chakra

Illustration 1 – The primary chakras

In recent years, and since the popularization of shamanic and psychedelic work in the West, several additional chakras have been added to this list:

8th chakra—usually describes the connection to Mother Earth (i.e., Pachamama or Gaia).
12th chakra—our connection to the Akashic records (i.e., where all the records and knowledge in the universe are stored).
13th chakra—where our contracts with other beings are written and stored for this lifetime.

I cannot tell you whether chakras exist or not. Some of them, such as the 12th and 13th, sound very exotic and somewhat out-of-fiction. However, the discussion of whether these centers exist or not is irrelevant. The chakras are symbolic tools that can be used to facilitate work. Individuals who engage in spiritual work, in meditation, and with medicine often have visceral sensations and experiences in these areas. For me, it is enough to use these areas as tools in inner work. In addition, at times, even conceptual, cognitive, and emotional work can be very beneficial while dealing with chakras.

For example, Sandy, a female in her 30s, was very angry with her mother, who had always shown extreme dependency in their relationship. Sandy was disappointed and upset that she had to care for her mother emotionally from a very young age. When introduced to the idea of the 13th chakra, she became interested in exploring the "contract" she had with her mother: "The contract should have been 'You'll take care of me when I'm a child, and I'll take care of you when you're old and I'm an adult.' But you didn't! You violated the contract. So now, I want to insert changes in the contract. My new contract with you is 'I don't owe you anything anymore. I do not need to protect you or care for you.'"

This was a steppingstone for Sandy to examine letting go of anger and gradually finding a place where she could forgive her mother and move on with her life.

We can think of the chakras as somatic centers (areas that we can sense) and, at times, conceptual points of reference for certain aspects and expressions of our being. As chakras begin to open, it is like new sense organs come online. New information, feelings, and insights begin to flow into consciousness, and sometimes this process can be disorienting and confusing.

Although I was originally educated and felt attracted to the seven-chakra system depicted above, my experience of these centers frequently did not correspond to confined descriptions. In my experience, I identify the following chakras as energetic centers in the psychic body, which we can use as portals to deeper aspects of our being. These locations are not always associated with the following descriptions, but I see some consistency in the expression of those "locations."

Although I give a few pointers to develop your acquaintance with chakras, I find it crucial to work with a teacher in person or follow a protocol (e.g., a retreat or a specific tradition) that has been formalized and utilized successfully by others. Opening these portals can occur spontaneously, especially in medicine work, and it is important for guide, therapist, and client to understand what is happening and how to work with the content that begins to stream into us.

CROWN—THE 7TH CHAKRA

Most people are not aware of their crown chakra. Interestingly, if you ever touched a human infant's head, you would become aware of the fontanels, two major soft spots on the top of the skull where the bone formation is not complete. The flexibility of the skull allows for a smoother transition in the birth canal, as the infant skull often gets elongated and squeezed during birth. The crown, although not located in physical reality, is situated at the top of the head around the area where the top soft spot lies.

The crown is often regarded as a portal to the aspect of the divine. That is consciousness itself and its empty nature specifically. Spiritual practices that focus on the crown and include visualization, mantra recitation, and somatic sensation often increase the crown's sensitivity to sensation. Simply direct your attention to that area in meditation and see how the experience unfolds. In Tibetan culture, even nonpractitioners would regularly receive training to open this region in preparation for death. Dying, they would practice Phowa (i.e., a practice from Tibetan Buddhism referred to as transference of consciousness) and release their consciousness into the nature of mind through the crown chakra.

Following meditation practice and, at times, medicine work, the crown will open, and a somatic experience usually follows. The somatic sensation of an opening of the crown can feel as gentle as a small flower opening on your head, a sense of expansion, or spreading. Sometimes it can feel like someone put a yarmulke on the top of your head, and sometimes it can feel like a fire blazing from the top of your head to the heavens.

The crown chakra is often regarded as an opening to the empty aspect of consciousness, namely Shiva in nondual Shaiva tantra. Sensation in this area is often accompanied by subtle or powerful spiritual experiences, including downloads, channeling, clarity, insights, access to other dimensions of reality, and perceptual shifts such as

1. Awareness of the Now (i.e., the timelessness of the moment)
2. Total conscious emptiness as the field in which all manifests, from which all manifests, and into which all dissolves
3. Unity consciousness—since everything is consciousness, the somatic realization of no separation arises. All is One. One is All.

THE THIRD EYE—THE 6ᵀᴴ CHAKRA

This is the portal of inner vision. When you close your eyes, can you visualize an apple? What color is it? The third eye is the organ of inner vision. Of course, there is a neurological system that corresponds to the ability to visualize objects, but the third eye is both the basis and expansion of that ability.

With practice and experience, you can notice the difference between visualizing reality according to your wishes versus "seeing" things that come to you. In addition, there is a unique sensation of a location between the eyebrows and the center of the forehead. It is subtle but unmistakable.

Jade was a failure to launch at 23 years old. At 18, he managed to get to college for one year and then left, went back home, closed the door, and started playing video games in his room, alone. That was five years ago. In his case, the diagnosis was really beneficial: autism spectrum disorder, high functioning. He had never been properly diagnosed. I am the guy who gets to tell people that they have it. He was relieved to know. The reason I am bringing Jade up is because he had absolutely no inner vision. He could not, for the love of god, visualize anything. Hypnosis, cannabis, and other psychedelics had no effects. This has a name: aphantasia.

From an energetic perspective, you could say that Jade had a "blocked third eye" or even worse, a "collapsed" one, as we say. I never found out why. He stopped coming shortly after the autism diagnosis made sense and sank in. That was the box he always needed to tick, and now life made sense. So maybe the diagnosis was not that beneficial after all? We never know how a client will take sincere attempts to help.

Activation in the third eye is usually associated with visions. Visions are often seen as mystical phenomena, but they are actually much more common than you may realize. In contrast with visualizing an object, a vision is something that comes to you, like a dream. Did you decide on the content of your dream from last night, or did it come to you?

There are many methods to develop acquaintance with the third eye, but what's common to them all is to become increasingly aware of the apparatus itself. Back to the apple. Close your eyes and keep looking at the apple, but pay more attention to the space in which it appears, the screen on which you see it. Change the color of the apple. The screen is still there. Put a white background behind the apple, fill all the space with white. The screen is still there. It's invisible. You can even keep your eyes open, read these words, and see the apple, but it will be more difficult to notice the inner screen on which it appears. It is difficult to notice when you have another visual perception. Close your eyes and visualize the apple. Notice the screen on which you perceive it; that is your third eye. Become intimate with it.

As you become more aware of the third eye, it is useful to sense the middle of the forehead or point near that between your eyebrows as a somatic reminder for inner vision. Focusing on this area can increase its sensitivity. As your sensitivity increases, you will more spontaneously remember to pay attention to what is projected on the screen of consciousness.

The development of this ability is different for each person in both content and context. For me, in the beginning, the visions included geometric patterns (almost like in psychedelic experiences but with less color and clarity). Later on, random faces of people I have never met started streaming in, then complete scenes from parts of life that I could not remember.

In my experience, a blocked third eye is often associated with focusing on what we want to see, or what we permit ourselves to see, rather than what is. The third eye's degree of openness is correlated with the degree of that which we are willing to see. How much are we allowing visions and experiences to come to us rather than seeking a particular perspective on reality?

If awareness is focused as a ray in the direction of positive or negative experiences based on our expectations and desires, we are limited to that band of the spectrum. If the ray of awareness is open, true visions and communication can manifest in our field of experience more fully and rapidly.

THROAT—THE 5TH CHAKRA

This is the portal of expression. The throat chakra symbolizes our ability to communicate, self-expression, and creativity. The degree to which we can authentically communicate is dependent on the access we have to the throat and the heart chakras. It is important to note that self-expression is not limited to verbal expression. A variety of art forms, dancing, building, making music, and working with your hands are all forms of self-expression. When the throat chakra is open and flowing, self-expression is fluid and there is a capacity to communicate with ourselves and others.

On the other hand, a blocked throat chakra can manifest as underexpressing ourselves in cases where not enough energy flows to this region. This is often noted with individuals who tend to overutilize "um," "you know," "people say," and similar phrases of speech. A blocked throat chakra in which there is too much energy circulating, but not appropriately manifesting, appears as overtalking, talking over others (i.e., focusing on hearing oneself speak), circumlocution, providing too many details, and struggling to make a point.

A collapsed throat chakra often takes the form of individuals who do not speak in public and use a very quiet tone or a high-pitched voice. When this condition is very acute or chronic, somatic symptoms begin to occur. These include chronic throat infections, acid reflux, and thyroid issues.

Interventions that can assist in clearing the throat chakra, in addition to energetic manipulation, can include engaging in art forms, public-speaking training, acting and dancing (I love sending clients to improv classes), gardening, and psychotherapy under the influence of hypnosis and other disinhibiting techniques.

HEART—THE 4TH CHAKRA

The heart chakra's main function is to feel emotions. It is the seat of authenticity. Your throat might express your truth, but your truth is "located" in your heart. You can become aware of it in your heart. The chocolate taste is in your mouth, but knowing that you like it is in your heart chakra.

The heart chakra covers the chest and has a lot of interesting aspects. One way to visualize the heart chakra is to imagine a flower opening in your chest. Usually in chakra visualization, the flowers of the chakras are imagined facing up or down, but for the sake of this specific explanation, it can be beneficial to imagine the flower facing out. The petals of the flowers represent different flavors of emotions (e.g., sadness, fear, joy, excitement, curiosity, disgust, anger, and so on). The pollinated center of the flower represents the ability to feel and utilize the spectrum of emotions. The stem of the flower is called the back of the heart.

Sensations of the heart chakra often occur at the center of the chest (the center point between the nipples). Sometimes the sensation takes place at the solar plexus or precisely on the frontal merging point of the rib cage.

The back of the heart is usually the least accessible area of this chakra. The stem of the flower is a portal (almost like a white hole) pouring energy into your chest from behind you. This energy causes your heart chakra petals to vibrate with the different emotional tones of your life. The back of the heart often symbolizes the ability to trust love, trust others, be okay with disappointments, accept all feelings, and be free to experience the world as it is, trusting that it is going to be okay no matter what happens.

HARA—COMBINING CHAKRAS 2 (SACRAL) AND 3 (SOLAR PLEXUS)

There is a lot going on in the belly from an energetic perspective. Different systems have various points of interest there. Japanese Zen and its offspring tend to focus on the lower dantien, about four fingerbreadths below the navel. The Indians have several chakras in the area, for example, the Manipura chakra, which is three fingerbreadths above the navel.

My current experience does not lead me to localize a particular location for energetic manifestations in the belly. There is so much there. When I use the term hara, I refer to the entire belly region from the solar plexus to the top of the pelvis. The hara is a primary portal considered to be the center of the mind, the body's center of gravity, and a gateway through which energy enters our body.

Issues with the hara often present as a lack of vitality in life, procrastination (all the energy is wasted on digestion and energy is stuck in loops that require a lot of digestion), difficulty enjoying life, or living life in cycles of pleasure and guilt (the unstoppable donut at 2 a.m. and the accompanying self-disgusted expression).

There is a complicated relationship in the hara between pleasure and pain, love and hate, love and betrayal, in and out. It is a protected area, often very uncomfortable to deal with at the beginning of deep work, and usually met with a lot of resistance.

The work there is not for beginners, although it is sometimes already happening when the client walks through the door. Gradual awakening at the hara level without preparation can be very unpleasant. Chronic pains, irritable bowel syndrome (IBS), chronic infections, indigestion, obesity, eating disorders, and fertility problems—it is all hara.

There are interventions I recommend for the hara when the time is right:

1. Martial arts to strengthen the energy field and the various sub-chakras, increase one's sensitivity in the belly region, and increase confidence, which can assist us in moving onward when times are hard.
2. Guided meditations focused on the hara with a very compassionate and openhearted approach are very beneficial, gentle inquiries.
3. Somatic work when ready and there is trust built with a good therapist. This can be done in somatic experiencing, yoga massage, Hakomi, embodied parts work, energy work, and, simplest of all, with a gentle and supportive hand resting on the belly.

4. Psychedelic medicine. Mushrooms and ayahuasca especially are masters at clearing energy in the entire body. Both are consumed by eating and drinking, and both have their effects on the digestive system as well. I have not experienced ayahuasca. A close friend and highly respected therapist told me, "It felt like a mechanical hand was moving things inside my body. It was rearranging things in me that were very messy. It was amazing." Mushrooms, in my experience, are somewhat gentler, but still, there is a definite movement and energetic composting that can take its toll in the belly.

ROOT—THE 1ST CHAKRA

The root chakra is associated with existence. It is, in some way, where Shakti manifests matter; our earthly connection, the place where the body begins; and where bodies create bodies. It is sexual, erotic, and dark like a cave deep in the earth, in which the shadows of creation are alive and kicking.

The root chakra is located in the general area of the pelvic floor, anus, and the genitals. Some traditions actually describe it as residing beneath the physical body, so beneath the pelvic floor, hanging there underneath the body.

One way to feel into the root chakra is to think of an immediate feeling of "I exist!" following waking up from a nightmare or general anesthesia. There is a new breath that rushes into your body as you wake up with shock and surprise to find yourself alive. It is a fear-based state that is often associated with a sense of very subtle or sometimes painful gripping of the pelvic floor for both men and women. It is often also correlated to the tightening and clenching of the jaw and teeth.

Blockages in the first chakra are often associated with fear, existential threats, and uncertainty. These can manifest as intense anxiety, panic attacks, hypervigilance (e.g., a very erratic and defensive biofield), muscle knots, pain and restricted movement in the pelvic floor and genital area, and digestive problems.

If the root is open, there is a state of flow and openness in life. There is a deep somatic trust in life, a trust in being that extends beyond life and death. There is a deep feeling of relaxation and somatic sensations of bliss.

PALMS AND FEET

Palms and feet are technically considered to be sub-chakras. There are dozens of sub-chakras in the psychic body, and many are important. However, the palms and feet often present various blockages or stuck energy. The palms are associated with our power of expressing ourselves in the world by creating, caring, and destroying. Arthritis in the palms or muscle knots can indicate a lot of activation or blockages in this area.

The feet represent our connection to Mother Earth. How stable do we feel standing on this planet? Is the earth holding us or are we holding ourselves? Are we able to receive energy, reassurance, and love deep from the core of the planet? Or do we feel separated and lost?

Additionally, there are kidney points at the soles of our feet that can be useful in medicine work to ground a client and help them center themselves and get out of their heads.

Meridians

Meridians often refer to pathways or channels in the body through which energy flows. The concept of meridians exists in various Eastern cultures: meridians in traditional Chinese medicine (TCM), Nadis in Ayurvedic medicine and Indian tantra (such as nondual Shaiva Tantra), keiraku in traditional Japanese medicine, and tsa in Tibetan medicine.

I chose to use the term meridians just out of personal preference, but any system will do. The world of meridians and energy manipulation justifies an entire book or encyclopedia. One can spend years studying this domain. I work closely with an acupuncturist who assists me in working with clients in diagnosing their chi (energy) flow and obstruction of specific meridians in the psychic body.

I find that a rudimentary understanding of the meridian system is important in deep work, but this can be accomplished in a relatively short time. This is because samskaras and other forms of energetic blockages often appear as a narrowing or, in some cases, almost complete blockage of the channels.

In medicine or breathwork journeys, blockages in meridians show up as sensations of pressure, pain, burning, tingling, or electric charges. In some of these cases, a guide can facilitate the process of release. A running joke among some guides is that they are energetic plumbers.

When a client senses a point of pain or contraction on the meridian, a gentle finger that traces the meridian from start to end can help bring awareness to the narrowing of the meridian and assist in releasing the blockage. Our awareness functions as the solvent agent that can melt energetic crystallization. You will also notice with time that activation of one point on the meridian will trigger an activation on the meridian in a different point of the body. For example, as energy moves and activates sensation in the bladder meridian in the neck, it could also be felt and manipulated at the end of the lateral little toe on the respective side of the body. These sensations can be used by a skilled guide as a map of possible blockages and for energetic manipulation, including extraction.

TCM and other traditions at times ascribe certain emotional aspects to meridians when those are open versus blocked. For example, the bladder meridian is associated with courage and the physical and emotional capacity to act when open. However, when this meridian is narrowed or blocked, it is associated with sensations of fear and terror. In my personal experience, the emotional aspects of meridians sometimes hit the spot and sometimes miss it entirely. I would rather inquire about what a client is actually experiencing emotionally at any given time rather than define the somatic experience for them. This further facilitates a process of exploration and curiosity rather than repeating an algorithmic superimposition of a concept that does not always resonate with subjective experience.

Here are some of the important meridians to remember in the human body that I often find are activated in meditation and medicine work:

1. Pancreas/Spleen
2. Stomach
3. Lung
4. Large Intestine
5. Kidney
6. Bladder
7. Liver

8. Gallbladder
9. Heart
10. Small Intestine
11. Triple Warmer

Common Energetic Presentations in Deep Work

In my work with people, over time, I have noticed several energetic presentations corresponding to various psychological and spiritual blocks. The following describes some of the crucial presentations often seen in deep work.

DISEMBODIMENT

In some cases of severe trauma, people can present with a psychic body that appears to be thrown "out" of the physical body temporarily when triggered or, more rarely, permanently dissociated from the physical body.

Ben, a male in his mid-40s, arrived with a recommendation for deep work when other forms of psychotherapy had failed. He presented as a bad case of a classic nice guy. He had amicably divorced five years previously, had been sober for six years, was a good father, had great relationships with his children, and was now two years into a new romantic relationship and going strong. He came to me because of abandonment anxiety. He was terrified that his new girlfriend was going to leave him. Turns out that his abandonment issues had been going on his entire life. His father abandoned him and his mother at a young age, and Ben transferred this fear to the archetype of the feminine.

The part of Ben that had to be silenced was the one that was screaming "SAVE ME!" In his pleading to women, attempting to make them appreciate him deeply and never leave him, he was trying to create an environment that would facilitate someone finally coming to the rescue. Then it would potentially be safe enough to share how fucked up he really was. People can smell that from miles away. They interpret it as a weakness, and biologically speaking, humans see weakness as an undesirable characteristic. So, Ben, despite his most positive capacities and the fact that he was a strong man, was perceived to be weak by all of his girlfriends, who were all of a certain

90

type and eventually broke up with him. He always, of course, remained a great friend to his exes. How could you let someone like that go?

If only Ben could once and for all admit that he needed rescue. If only he could voice it truly and authentically, speaking with the voice of an emotionally buried part (i.e., a samskara), a part that wanted to find that voice in the energetic, impenetrable prison that enfolded it. But he could not. Not with CBT, EMDR, somatic experiencing, or hypnotherapy. His ego defenses were too powerful.

A 45-minute session of holotropic breathwork produced an intense somatic release. There was no accompanying episodic or insightful content, but nevertheless, something significant in the body was released. In the following two weeks, he felt a sense of being better connected to himself and others.

Two weeks after his breathwork session, Ben had an MDMA journey with a guide. In his session, Ben had another major release. He saw the moment he broke his femur in a car accident when he was fourteen. He was injured so badly that he had to be airlifted to emergency surgery. His life was in danger.

While lying on a stretcher, waiting for the medevac in pain, terror, and shock, he discovered "the switch" and turned it on. He remembered that he actually invented the switch when he was a small child, the day his father left. He got into the closet, closed the door, and disappeared from his body. His parents were still fighting in the background, but it could not get to him. "I was over it." He was able to create what appeared to be a very effective separation in his psyche between himself and unwanted experiences. Little did he know that his switch was a factory of samskaras that were sitting and waiting in his psychic body for their inevitable release (usually physical death for most people).

Ben's surgery was successful, saving his life and leg, but recovery was complicated and long. Not only did he not get a room for himself, but he was placed in a recovery room with the decimating body of a ten-year-old boy who was dying of cancer. The boy's family would come every day to the room and spend the entire day in fear, terror, and grief with their son and sibling, dying with him. Ben could not be rescued. His parents could not hear his unspoken screams. He had to be strong. Plus, he had the switch. So, it got turned on and remained on for a long time. Then he found booze . . .

Ben is doing well now. Life continues, but he is whole and interfaces with reality in an authentic way, respecting his strengths and struggles. Ben's entire psychic body was thrown out of his physical body for a significant duration of time due to chronic states of helplessness and hopelessness (i.e., the learned helplessness model). In his regular life, this looked like significant numbness in the body, lack of movement in the legs (as was presented during his intense breathwork session), being a terrible dancer, lacking rhythm, and lacking caring for massage or good food. Basically, he was out of sync due to consciousness abiding in a higher vibrational frequency that did not resonate with the vibrational frequency of the physical body.

Once Ben became conscious of the switch, he could understand the consequences of using it and the obstacles it created in his life. Once he was able to release the switch, he had a direct pathway to explore his wounded child and other inner parts that needed attention and an intimate, loving relationship.

CONSTRICTED MERIDIANS

When a meridian becomes constricted, there are usually very specific somatic presentations. In my case, these were chronic infections in both my ears (gallbladder meridian). What I have observed in clients and from discussions with colleagues is that inflamed meridians often present as rashes in specific areas, a very tight muscle group, chronic muscle knots in specific locations, allergies, food sensitivities, digestive problems, and so on and so forth.

I was surprised to see Jen enter my office using a cane. On the phone, she sounded young, healthy, and strong. She was an attractive female in her 30s, but nevertheless, she was using a cane to walk and grimaced in pain while sitting down on the blue couch. Three months previously, Jen had standard knee replacement surgery due to an injury. Following the surgery, she experienced severe inflammation that left her incapable of using her dominant right leg. She lost her job and became depressed. In addition to her disability, she was experiencing chronic and relentless nerve pain.

There was no cure in sight. Her physicians diagnosed her pain as nerve damage, prescribed aggressive painkillers, and suggested nerve blocks and more surgeries. The medications and other interventions did not work. Mindfulness and other forms of alternative approaches (even acupuncture) also did not ameliorate her condition.

Jen had a lot of childhood trauma. She was severely physically, sexually, and emotionally abused by family members, friends, and strangers in various periods of her life. She had gone through CBT, EMDR, and somatic experiencing, which saved her life and helped her stay sober on occasion. In addition to all the fear, grief, and sadness that was waiting to pour out of her poor body, anger and, most importantly, hot and pure rage were sitting there, waiting to explode.

The liver meridian is often associated with the suppression and holding of rage. I did ask you not to blindly accept the emotional descriptions of meridians, but in Jen's case, it was spot on. The liver meridian going through her leg and knee was the precise pathway where the pain, hotness, and burning were sensed.

One psilocybin journey with a guide brought an immediate improvement. Give it to the mushrooms, they are true healers and incredible at digesting samskaras and removing blockages from meridians and chakras. The pain was almost gone, and Jen was able to begin exercising and build strength in her leg. She required another mushroom journey about six months later to consolidate the improvement and resolve additional samskaras that now had the space and permission to rise to the surface.

BLOCKED CHAKRAS

When chakras are partially or completely blocked, there is a pause or disruption in the function usually associated with that specific chakra. The way the disruption manifests can vary significantly from case to case, but the common thread is disruption to the basic function of the energy center.

The heart and the first chakra (pelvic floor) often present with very common blockages, and almost everyone has obstructions in these areas. Blockages in the heart chakra usually revolve around control of emotion (associated with pain and heaviness in the heart and stiffness and numbness throughout the extremities) and of reality (associated with stiffness, pain, and rigidity in the neck, arms, jaw, and shoulders, and neurological symptoms in the hands and fingers).

In my case, due to the trauma that I sustained in childhood, I blocked my heart chakra unconsciously but purposefully to protect myself. The grief for my father was too much to feel, too overwhelming, so I closed my heart to some extent. I still had emotions, but I was uncomfortable feeling them. There was a sense of rigidity and control in the way I carried myself around. "Feel less. Allow less." These were the statements running unconsciously in my OS.

Blockages in the first chakra are usually associated with fear, existential threats, and uncertainty.

In his childhood, Bill used to go with his unpredictable father to the beach. His eccentric dad would go swimming in the stormy ocean for a long time. Bill, who was terrified of losing his father, would stand on the beach trying to spot his father's head popping between the waves.

He told me during a guided meditation focused on the pelvic floor and hara, "It's so tight down there! I never noticed how tight it was. I remember now when my dad would go swimming in the stormy ocean. I stood there on the beach, and I was terrified that he would never come back, that I would have to go home to my barely functioning mother. I was trying to make myself higher by standing on my tippy toes so that I could see better. But the sand was deep, and I couldn't get a grip. I squeezed so hard in my pelvic floor to try to make myself taller and higher. The fear squeezed it, and it never really released."

It did release, but it needed medicine and deep work. Bill's pelvic floor then descended in a good way.

In some cases where the blockage of a chakra is complete, some in the field might use the term "imploded chakra." This refers to a state in which the chakra is very stagnant, almost not moving at all. There is very little sensation, and the person usually describes a sense of intense emotional numbing, such as "I don't feel anything."

Jeremy was a good-looking and compassionate male pediatrician in his early 30s. He lost his younger brother when he was seven years old. His father abandoned him and his mother and, not much later, died from a heart attack. Finally, Jeremy's mother was now dying of cancer, and he was about to be alone in this world with no surviving family members.

"I just want to cry, but I can't get it out. Sometimes in therapy, if I have a good moment, I can get a tear out, but I need to sob! I can feel it. It's stuck in my throat!"

Jeremy's throat chakra was definitely blocked to some extent, but his heart chakra had completely collapsed in the total sadness, loss, and destruction that he endured. He was smart, meditated, went to therapy, and was motivated. But he could not progress.

One MDMA journey with a good guide was all it took to crack the energetic concrete. Then the work could really begin.

Holding Energy for Others

If you have children, you know of their sponge-like nature. If you do not have children, you might have dogs or cats. Have you noticed that your pets tend to take on your personality and habits? From an absolute perspective, there is no separation between us and others. But even from a relative perspective, our psychic body is not solid. Its boundaries are permeable. The more open and awakened you are, the more permeable these boundaries are. Permeability is what allows the exchange of information, feelings, and ideas. When we do not have self-awareness or have limited awareness of the potency of emotions and interpersonal communication, we do not monitor the exchanges of energy between us and others. Go back to the last fight you had with your partner, a parent, or a good friend. You might be able to remember the sensation of anger that your partner "gave" you. You were not angry until they came over and dumped their stuff all over you. "Dad came home angry from work and contaminated the entire house with his nerves and irritation. Now we are all pissed off. Even the dog."

As children, we are powerless to notice what and how we absorb energetic phenomena and raw emotions from our parents. There are many studies about maternal depression and its effects on infants and toddlers and about paternal anxiety and anger and their effects on the acting-out behaviors and oppositionality of elementary school-age children. We helplessly love our parents dearly despite their imperfections and terrifying sides. We want to help them.

Children intuitively know that they can "pull" negative energy from their parents. In psychology, we call this "empathy," the ability to sense and feel what another person feels by using our mirror neurons. In the energy world, this can be referred to as the process of absorbing and holding energy for others.

Holding energy for others can be directed to a specific person or more collective energetic patterns that we internalize. As an example of the former, Abraham sat up in the middle of an MDMA journey caressing his lower back and asking his guide to place his hands on his kidneys: "There is something going on there. I don't know what it is. Help me."

The guide provided him with a light, gentle touch and asked Abraham to go deeper into that region, into his kidneys, and allow any sensation or thought to flower in his mind, including nothing at all.

Within a few seconds, Abraham said, "It's my mom. It's not even mine, it's my mother's fear. She was so scared, so terrified, so anxious. I didn't know that I took that from her. I tried to help her keep it together. I wanted so much for her to feel relaxed and happy. It's so heavy there."

The guide asked, "Do you still want to hold it for her?"

"NO!" said Abraham. "I wasn't holding it for her. I was holding it for me. I can't help her anymore."

Abraham and the guide were able to release a great deal of energy via extraction (which will be discussed momentarily), positive affirmation, and further deep psychotherapy in later sessions. Abraham described the sensation of letting the energy go as "losing 60 pounds I never knew I carried."

Chelsea, a smart atheist software engineer, struggled with pain in the hara throughout her entire psilocybin journey. Her female guide did all she could to help her move the energy in the body, but Chelsea struggled to let it go. She was ruminating and stuck in loops in her mind. A couple of hours into the journey, a song with a prayer to the divine mother came up on the playlist. Chelsea felt the constriction of her bra and, as she felt comfortable with her guide, moved to remove her bra and remain semi-naked on the mat. She felt liberated and even asked for aromatic oil ointment to be gently applied over her back and throat. The song began to make her emotional. She sat up, rocked with the music, tears streaming down her face. This was not the Chelsea that usually came to my office, the rigid, stiff, well-dressed, and heady person I enjoyed playing mental chess games in my fruitless attempts to move through her ego defenses.

After several minutes of gentle rocking and crying, Chelsea said to her guide in sudden surprise, "It's all the women. All the sadness and anger that women hold as a group. All the fear and anger for what men have done to us. It is all in my body, in my guts. I can feel it. I need to make peace with that. It is tormenting me every single day."

And she did. Chelsea could not resolve the effects of systematic patriarchy over the feminine. However, she could face the feelings she had about them and stop defending herself from the anger and grief that were waiting in her psychic body for her to acknowledge and digest them. Once she did, she did not have to pretend anymore that pain and angst were a part of her inner world. She better connected to her source of power and confidence, and her interpersonal relationships (including with men) became more intimate and fulfilling.

Energetic Manipulation

You cannot properly learn how to work with energy from a book. But I can point you in the right direction and speak about possible venues for working with energy. I highly recommend studying and experimenting with various energetic modalities to see what works best for you. These can include hatha yoga, Reiki, acupuncture, touch work, breathwork, mantra recitation, visualization, and more.

When do we want to work with energy?

1. When a client is stuck in therapy. Some individuals can be very heady and evasive, going through loops in their minds without getting deeper into themselves. The therapist can encourage energetic flow in the body (via breathing, meditation, and touch) and trigger samskaras or obstructions of chakras and meridians. This brings to the conscious surface emotions, memories, or guardians (i.e., psychological parts) that need to be addressed.

2. When energy is stuck in a particular location or meridian. This often occurs in medicine journeys but can also be experienced in a regular session when alternate states of consciousness are introduced (e.g., hypnosis or guided meditation). The guide and therapist can help "move" the energy, increasing the sensation of flow, and the journey can continue, allowing release and additional content to arise from the unconscious.

Regardless of the modality you choose to learn to work with energy, there are three fundamental principles common to any work with energetic phenomena:

1. Energy constantly streams into our body from the beyond. As long as we have a physical body, there is a flow, a refreshing river that attempts its best to enter our body, feed us, and vitalize us with new experiences and essence.

2. Energy that enters our body will eventually attempt to go back to the source to be united with the ground of being. However, it is often blocked or slowed down in the folds of consciousness due to compulsive self-referencing, narrowing of meridians, blocked chakras, and samskaras.

3. Awareness itself is the most powerful dissolving agent that can melt energetic crystallizations, blockages, narrowing of meridians, and samskaras. Hence, the capacity to feel into, sense, and experience energy blockages in our body is what releases them back to the source.

The following are specific interventions that can assist in the release of energy. In essence, each one of these approaches increases the client's subjective awareness of energy processes and facilitates their release.

EXTRACTION

There are long-lasting traditions of individuals carrying "dark" or bad energy in their bodies. The traditions of cleansing energy and entities out of people's bodies exist both in the West (e.g., exorcism) and in indigenous cultures (e.g., Mazatec and Tibetan). For me, it does not matter if it is "real" or imagined. A client who feels and thinks they are possessed or carrying dark energy in their body experiences it as real. In such cases, a ceremony of extracting energy can be very beneficial in helping them move on with their life and achieve a feeling of freedom, which facilitates their working on layers of being that were previously obscured from view.

The extraction of energy does not necessarily have to be esoteric. It can be as simple as lighting a candle, a source of cleansing smoke (e.g., sage, palo santo), offering a prayer, or maybe brushing a body part using a hand or a feather. The act is symbolic in nature. If this is something you are interested in, I suggest learning it from an actual teacher.

BREATHWORK

To make a comparison to plumbing, extraction is the removal of an obstruction in the pipe, and breathwork is putting so much energy into the system that it will powerfully wash the inside of the channels and push obstructions not overly integrated into our identity out.

This can be painful and difficult in some cases but is very effective with unidentified blockages. The block of "I'm not good enough," for example, is not a good candidate to be ameliorated by breathwork, as it is integrated into our identity, whereas held and unprocessed anger or sadness that was previously too overwhelming to be digested (i.e., samskaras) is a good candidate for this approach.

If you are interested in this approach, I recommend learning the Wim Hof Method, holotropic breathwork, pranayama, or kundalini yoga.

AWARENESS

There are several spiritual and psychotherapeutic modalities that involve a somatic focus. As these approaches increase the conscious experience of the psychic body and its various parts, they help gradually melt and move energy that is stuck and obstructed. Tantra and its various offspring (e.g., nondual Shaiva tantra, Dzogchen, Bon, Mahamudra, and yoga) are wonderful and creative ways to work with somatic and energetic blockages.

Psychotherapeutically, I can recommend Hakomi and somatic experiencing, which both incorporate awareness and/or touch for moving energy while deeply supporting the client.

WORKING WITH TOUCH

In stark contrast to what I was taught in my classical psychology schooling and clinical settings, touch is an essential part of good psychotherapy for a variety of reasons. However, let me be very clear: despite the intimacy that I am about to encourage, this touch has nothing to do with sexual touch. I feel compelled to say this, as I personally know of many inappropriate sexual encounters and examples of touch between guides, therapists, and clients.

In or outside the room, a guide, sitter, or therapist must never have sex with a client. You never massage their pelvic floor or come close to their vagina, anus, penis, nipples, or lips. A guide or therapist (who does not specialize in sexual work and have a specific sexual contract with their client) does not touch clients in a sexual manner. Period.

We use touch for several reasons:

1. To assess. In the beginning, without physical touch at all, you can just look at someone and notice how open they are to touch. The stiff ones are hiding a lot. But the soft ones are sometimes monsters in disguise. You never know. Touch says a lot.
2. To love. All the people we work with feel deprived of love, primarily self-love. And although their need is a black hole that knows no end, giving them, at least for a short time, a touch of tenderness is equal to the healing of many talk sessions. A good massage can bring a lot of emotions out of people.

3. To move energy. Touch can help move energy by focusing attention. A hand on the heart can help a client not feel alone and direct their attention to the sensation of love, with our hands reflecting that love back to them. They project their energy onto us, and we radiate it back to them with the hand. Movement of energy can happen on a chakra or on a meridian. Do not touch the meridians and chakra close to the genitals, but direct the client's attention to these regions verbally.

4. To help release a samskara. Samskaras can be located anywhere in the body. Their release can be expressed through various means, for example, cramping in the hands, locked jaw, shakes, burning sensations, etc. Touch can help to distract or attenuate some of these experiences.

I advise you to learn how to touch. You can learn somatic experiencing, although I find it a bit complicated and overly commercialized. At the end of the day, touch is a simple and straightforward process. All it requires is gentle, loving hands and meeting another person in the need for intimacy beyond sexuality. An additional modality that I like is the Tamura Method (*http://tamuramethod.com/*), but I am sure there are many more that I know nothing about. Go and learn.

MEDICINE

The most powerful energetic healers and manipulators are the various medicines that can be used in a psychedelic journey. Organic entheogens (i.e., mushrooms, cacti, ayahuasca) not only move, digest, and clean energy but are also intelligent teachers that can teach us about energy. This is most beneficial when working with samskaras and obstructions that are integrated into our identities. The teachers can help us to see reality from very different perspectives, dislodging the deep identification that we can develop with certain energetic blocks: "I'm not good enough," "I'm unworthy of love," "Life is difficult," "Humanity is evil," and so on and so forth.

I do not personally have much experience with ayahuasca (i.e., DMT) or cacti (i.e., mescaline) but do have extensive experience with mushrooms in my own healing. Mushrooms are truly benevolent healers and incredible at digesting samskaras and removing blockages from meridians and chakras.

In a journey, the release and energetic work conducted by a medicine is not always cognitive. Sometimes it will be pure sensation, with no explanation of why and what this is related to. Sometimes it is accompanied by images and insights. It is hard to predict. The guide's role in such situations is to help the client experience this without having to understand everything.

Also, synthetic medicine can be extremely potent in moving energy and removing obstructions. 5-MeO-DMT can shoot the obstructions straight out of your body. I personally experienced the removal of two main obstructions from my crown and heart chakra with this medicine. MDMA and ketamine are also very powerful in moving energy when used correctly.

Due to the potency of psychedelic medicines, the presentation of energetic phenomena in journeys can be very powerful. This is especially the case with individuals who have significant trauma. Under the effects of medicine, the spectrum of energetic release and processing is wide and can include the following:

- shakes and trembling all over the body, but mostly in the extremities and legs
- pain focused in a particular region
- convulsions
- a deep sense of relief (e.g., "I feel like I lost 60 pounds")
- sensations of burning hands or feet
- intense pressure
- tight jaw (especially when resistance is present)
- belching and farting
- vomiting and purging (often purging only air, as there is no actual content in the stomach)
- bleeding

Unlocked Memories

I would like to say a few words about unlocking memories and visions in deep work. I often get questions from clients like "What I saw on the journey, what I see in dreams, what I saw in meditation, is it all real or am I just making it up?" "Did my father really rape me or not?" "Did I kill someone or not?" "Did I really speak to god or am I just making it up?"

I don't know.

There are many studies about the accuracy of retrieved memories, which don't look good. Apparently, from the perspective of the physical brain, we change memories every time we recall them. From the spiritual perspective, all is mind and, therefore, nothing you recall ever really happened. At the moment of "recall," reality is actually recreated differently, as a memory rather than an event.

The degree of truth in the memory is irrelevant. What matters is that we experience a specific vision, perception, insight, or remembrance. The reason we experience the content in a specific way is because that is how the samskara found a way to release and express itself. I do not know if the samskara was created in this lifetime or a thousand years ago in Australia. I just know that, for whatever reason, something dormant came alive and is finding its blessed way out of you back to the source.

So, no, unlocked memories are not reliable at all. Yet, they are the clues to the path.

What to investigate and find is the truth of your heart.

The psychic body is a crucial element in deep work and healing. Sooner or later, we meet an invisible ceiling in self-development that hinders our progress. This obstacle is often the result of a lack of understanding of the bridge between body and mind. The model of the psychic body that I present here is that bridge between the body and mind, which appear at times to be separated but are actually points on a spectrum. Once we develop a better understanding of the psychic body, we can move to the basic skills required to work with deeper layers of our being.

In this chapter, what I have said about the psychic body and energy work is quite limited. I highly recommend seeking further education, a teacher, or a modality in which you can train to further your experience and knowledge.

CHAPTER 5

DEEP WORK
FOUNDATIONS

THERE IS A STRONG TREND TOWARD STANDARDIZING PSYCHEDELICS IN personal development and spiritual work. Plenty of people will encounter psychedelics over the next few years. If you are working in mental health or medical settings, one way or another, you are very likely to play a part in this massive wave of transformation. In this chapter, I describe the elements that I found to be very helpful in my and my clients' deep work resulting from psychedelic journeys and spiritual openings. I see the following elements as crucial foundations on which deep work can flourish without encountering too many obstacles.

Understanding of Pain and Suffering

Understanding the nature of pain and suffering is an organic process that becomes clearer, especially in psychedelic journeys. Some conceptual understanding of these is beneficial for all. Pain and suffering are *the* reasons that clients show up on my doorstep. Not a single person comes because they are bored or have too much money in their bank account. We show up when the pain and suffering we carry in our psyche is too much to bear. We engage in therapeutic or spiritual work in an attempt to escape or resolve pain and suffering.

Please understand: suffering is the engine of change. It is not something that needs to be resolved but rather a call to pay attention to what is truly the most important question: Who or what am I?

Pain will never stop. It is integral to the body. But it does not need to cause suffering. A scratch on my boy's knee at the age of three is the end of the world. It requires a Band-Aid, kisses, a hug, tears, reassurance, and sometimes a lollypop. As he matures, the same scratch at the age of seven still delivers the same amount of pain, but it does not hurt him as much. It does not threaten his existence.

Suffering is the story we tell ourselves about pain and who we are as the entity feeling the pain. It will never stop as long as there is an identification with the little "me." Understanding this conceptually is insufficient by itself to create change, but the conceptual framework can be viscerally experienced and reinforced in psychedelic journeys and meditation, which can then support us in transforming our relationship to whatever it is we suffer from.

SOMATIC KNOWING

How do you know when you are in love? How do you know if you like or hate eating liver? It is undeniable. You know it in your bones. We can call it intuition. However, in modern society, we often rely on conceptual understanding in order to verify something rather than trusting a gut feeling or a deeper sense of knowing. Training this ability requires engaging in meditation and therapy, and probably the biggest shift in this domain comes out of engaging in body awareness practice, somatic work, and psychedelic journeys directed at somatic experiencing of emotions and insights.

Attention Training—the Capacity to Sustain, Track, and Relax Attention

The average human's attention span is approximately eight seconds, and some studies have suggested that it has become significantly shorter in recent decades, decreasing by about 25 percent between 2000 and 2015, probably due to the proliferation of screens in our lives (Hays, 2015, Microsoft, 2015). People who have never trained their minds or, at the very least, received teaching about the functionality of the mind, are enslaved to a hydra, a monster with infinite heads. The "outside" world is brimming with objects of perception. There is so much to see, touch, and feel. The primary reason our attention skips so quickly is because we really want to touch and sense these objects. We truly believe they are real. It is the glitter of light and awe in my daughter's eyes as she enters Disneyland, which is real for her.

But the inside is just as rich. When we open ourselves to the inner world or inner space, we discover a new dimension of richness. You could be an atheist Silicon Valley engineer who has never had a single spiritual vision in life. Yet, five grams of psilocybin are likely to show you that an inner world exists beyond a shadow of a doubt. And that inner world is intelligent and conscious.

Think of attention as a muscle. There is a spectrum to the flexibility of that muscle, ranging from completely loose to completely tense.

A very weak muscle of attention is almost never consciously used. This is essentially the case in someone who can barely direct their attention. Almost any outside stimuli (e.g., a squirrel climbing up a tree) or thought (e.g., *I wonder what's for dinner*) pulls their attention and interest, like the MO of a four- to five-year-old. This is an obstacle in medicine work and meditation. Such individuals will absolutely benefit to some degree from deep work. They might have some energetic release, maybe a couple of insights, but there is also a greater risk of getting lost in the drama, the narrative, and belief in the experience because it's "real."

I find that most individuals with a very loose attention muscle, who are enslaved by their mind, show up in adulthood, once society no longer finds their carefree attitude and distractibility cute, with ego-dystonic thoughts and behaviors (that is, a "You are right, and I am wrong" approach to the world). They often find themselves to be "not good enough." They perceive the world to be constantly criticizing them and have a strict internal judge. Such individuals are often on a constant journey of becoming "good enough."

Upon encountering psychedelics, such a person can easily become distracted and lost in constant bombardment from the unconscious. People can become overwhelmed, and this might show up somatically or mentally. This is often perceived as feelings of terror, fear, the inability to close one's eyes, frequent visits to the bathroom, the constant need to change factors in the environment (e.g., music, clothes, smells, and light), and difficulty disengaging from interpersonal interactions (e.g., being hyperverbal and not letting go of the presence of the guide in the room.)

A control freak has a tight muscle of attention, like the hypervigilant Navy SEAL version of George Costanza. Such a person, due to intense existential fear or traumatic experiences, usually limits the range of experiences they permit in their subjective life. I had such a tight muscle. It creates a very narrow and focused ray of attention. Such individuals are often successful and have a gift in a skill or field, yet are lone wolves. Living life this way is exhausting, constricting, and controlling. Family members and friends of such individuals often feel "controlled" and dictated to with respect to how things should be and appear. They have tight control over feelings and behaviors, and any deviation from the plan is accompanied by psychological resistance that shows up in the form of stress, anger, frustration, and anxiety. Such individuals often exhibit ego-syntonic thoughts, feelings, and behaviors. This is an "I am right, you are wrong" approach to the world. They often find themselves to be leaders or wannabe leaders. They can be grandiose in their relationships with themself and others.

Upon meeting psychedelics, such a person often exhibits rigidity and a thick veil between consciousness and the unconscious. Many such individuals find themselves lying on the mat, ready to go, but still unconsciously holding the experience at arm's length. They are in their minds, trying to let go and surrender, only to meet with deep resistance in the body. In the room, this manifests as "I don't feel anything; I need more medicine," tightness and pain in the neck and jaw, and lack of internal vision (i.e., third-eye activation).

The balance of attention and the ability to shift that attention between focused and relaxed is very important for spiritual practice in general and working with psychedelics in particular.

In order for a muscle to function properly, it needs to be able to tighten, sustain an effort, and relax when appropriate. There is an intuitive knowing in the muscle, but often, it needs to learn timing and degrees of strength. Have you seen an infant learn to walk? It takes months for those muscles to coordinate and build the capacity to fall intentionally. This process needs to be applied to our ability to work with attention.

When properly used, focused attention can be an anchor that can help navigate an opening into an inner world as a result of a psychedelic session.

In contrast, often when working with psychedelics, there is also a need to "let go" and allow the medicine to take us wherever "it" needs to go. The ability to let go is dependent on trust in the medicine, the guide, and oneself. Attention must be taught to relax, and once it does, psychological and physiological resistance in deeper dimensions of consciousness is revealed spontaneously.

To train attention to focus and relax, I highly recommend engaging in a variety of meditative practices. Meditation is often seen as a practice to relax the body and mind. That is true, but there are many types of meditation aimed at developing different qualities. For example, meditation can involve practices such as visualization, meditation with and without an object, open awareness practices, body scans, and mantra recitation. For the beginner, deciding where and how to start working with meditation can be overwhelming. There are so many resources and teachers on YouTube alone that it can be confusing. I suggest, at least in the beginning, following an established tradition that has a proven history of producing realized beings (with all their human imperfections). Other teachers could be wonderful as well but might have an incomplete perspective considering the view described in this book. For example, Sam Harris, who is a wonderful teacher and has excellent guided meditation recordings, takes more of an aesthetic position, which I feel fits less closely with my own personal view. However, you are the author of your life. Whatever works for you is the best choice.

Below are various spiritual traditions that, in my opinion, offer a complete path of meditative practice. Some are more structured (e.g., Vipassana), others more open-ended (e.g., Zen). I suggest experimenting and seeing what works best for you. For me, I started with Dzogchen Semde, which I highly recommend as a structured approach to learning how to work with the mind, attention, movement of thoughts, and stillness. I later moved on to other approaches and combined different modalities in my work based on my needs and development.

If possible, I highly recommend getting a good foundation with the following traditions. Engagement in these traditions requires the guidance of a good teacher. Engaging with the practices of any of these traditions does not require one to convert or follow religious strictures. I recommend a process of experimentation to see what works for you. These traditions will overshoot the original goal of training the mind, take the practitioner much deeper in their process, and also address additional fundamental abilities described below that I find important in deep work.

DZOGCHEN SEMDE

Dzogchen, also known as Atiyoga, is considered to be one of the highest schools of tantra in Tibetan Buddhism and Yungdrung Bon. It is a complete path to total awakening and comprised of three series: Semde (mind series), Longde (space series focused on body postures and energetic work), and Menngagde (secret and direct instructions to recognize the nature of the mind and reality itself). This tradition was considered secret until several decades ago, and instructions were only given to advanced practitioners who completed a series of initial trainings (i.e., Ngöndro). More specifically, for the training of the attention and mind, Dzogchen Semde consists of a very powerful series of structured meditations and instructions. I highly recommend the following living masters with whom I have had the opportunity to study and learn: Lama Lena, Tenzin Wangyal Rinpoche, and Tsoknyi Rinpoche. Two other excellent teachers in this tradition under whom I have not had the opportunity to study are Khyentse Rinpoche and Mingyur Rinpoche.

NONDUAL SHAIVA TANTRA

Considered one of the roots, if not *the* root of, the path of tantra, this tradition emphasizes the realization of nondual consciousness as the ground and essence of reality. This path is associated with devotion to the union between Shiva (supreme consciousness) and Shakti (the spontaneous and intelligent dynamism of consciousness) and the embodiment of their union in physical reality. This tradition is abundant and quite recently appeared in the West after a rich history followed by centuries of decline in India. In this tradition, I highly recommend Christopher Wallis (also known as Hareesh) and Lawrence Edwards, with whom I have the opportunity to learn. Other famous teachers in this tradition include Sally Kempton, Paul Muller-Ortega, and Mark Dyczkowski, whom I do not know personally but who come highly recommended.

VIPASSANA

Also known as insight meditation, this is a group of practices related to the stream of Theravada Buddhism. A Vipassana retreat usually consists of a ten-day course starting at 4:30 a.m. and ending at 9:00 p.m. with about ten hours of meditation a day. This is hardcore and not an easy start. However, it will bring a significant change to one's ability to work with attention and the mind in a relatively short span of time.

MODERN NONDUAL APPROACHES

There are many modern teachers who emphasize the role of nondual consciousness. I had the opportunity to learn under the following highly recommended teachers: Adyashanti (*The End of Your World*), John Prendergast (*The Deep Heart*), and Eckhart Tolle (*The Power of Now*). I also highly recommend *True Meditation* by Adyashanti as a wonderful audio-guided meditation companion. *Inner Engineering* by Sadhguru is also recommended for exploring meditation and spirituality from a modern Indian yogi teacher.

Preferably, by the time an individual enters medicine work, I would like them to
- See thoughts
- Be able to differentiate between stillness and movement in the mind
- Have had a glimpse of the nature of mind

Shifts in Identity

Once we begin to discover inner space and the rich inner world of consciousness, there is an opportunity to see that identity is not as cohesive and real as we believe it to be. More specifically, as described earlier in the chapter "Ego," we can come to realize that our identity is composed of many psychological parts and personalities, some of which are more dominant than others. In one helpful model, over time, we can become aware of three major types of psychological "parts," as described by IFS:

Exiled parts—psychological identities that were found to be overwhelming and dangerous to the psyche and, therefore, got locked away in the depths of the unconscious.

Protectors—identities that guard consciousness from the appearance of an exiled part. Protectors often take the form of an inner critic, an internalized abuser, a wall, a rock, blackness, or a tyrant. In psychedelic journeys, they often take an archetypal form, like dragons (the protectors of the unconsciousness), insects, or other scary or revolting entities that make us turn away from an inward perspective and avoid diving deep inside.

Firefighters—psychological identities that emerge if forbidden and threatening content arises in consciousness. This is often experienced as suicidal tendencies, a need to shut down in depression, or distraction using substances and acting-out behaviors.

As we dive deeper into ourselves, we can also become aware that the various parts that compose our interface with the world manifest in a space called the Self. Discovery of this part of our being is crucial for deep work, as this is felt to be the core of who we are, beyond all the parts that are exiled and seeking safety. It is much easier and more beneficial to engage in this process of discovery with a therapist or guide. For this, I highly recommend a therapist who has trained in IFS. IFS is a psychotherapy model developed by Richard Schwartz that focuses on understanding and working with the different psychological "parts" or identities within an individual's mind. It fits right in with psychedelic-assisted psychotherapy and lubricates our understanding of reality and the ego.

One tool I find very beneficial in working with clients on identity shifts and discovering parts is John Bradshaw's book *Homecoming*. Even though this is an older book, I think that the guided meditations and exercises are effective and conducive to starting developing a deep relationship with our inner child and the ability to consider different aspects of ourselves. This can be a foundation to more complex parts work (via IFS) and the identification of samskaras in the psychic body associated with various self-images and undigested emotional content.

In summary, through investigating these and similar modalities, we come to experience that the culmination of the spiritual path is a fundamental shift in identity. Psychology and coaching usually seek a relative shift in one's identity, that is, "improving myself." Spiritually calls for a shift that crosses a threshold into the nondual black hole of no return. More specifically, the shift is from an individual with a name and personality into a more flexible identity of the entire universe, which sees and feels itself as itself. This "bigger" identity does not contradict the individual identity. There is an experience of reality from the dream-like perspective of an individual with a name and personality *combined with* the absolute perspective, as nonseparate things.

Prior Recognition of Extra-Conscious States

The "normal" state of consciousness that people experience in their waking life prior to awakening can be characterized as continually transfixed by objects of experience (i.e., inner objects such as thoughts and outer objects such as ice cream) or self-referential processes (e.g., "I'm awesome" or "I'm a piece of shit").

Extra-conscious states include out-of-body experiences, simulated death experiences (e.g., such as those which 5-MeO-DMT and ketamine can provide at times), synchronicity of senses, communication with beings beyond this "current" reality, and many states that would be considered in West European and American cultures as weird, eccentric, or substance-induced.

Recognition of such states outside of journeys is important in inducing the inner knowing that such states are obtainable without medicine. Moreover, every medicine has its own side effect profile and, grossly speaking, tends to reduce some aspects of clarity.

Experiencing extra-conscious states without the use of medicine usually entails a "cleaner" sense of clarity. That is not to say that medicine is not clean but to point out the difference between a state of consciousness that is sober and one that is high or drunk.

Clarity is very important in this kind of work. In a journey, the medicine has a lot of power in deciding where and how the journey will unfold. You essentially give a spirit, a nonhuman teacher, permission to enter your psychic body and take control of portions of the dashboard for a while. Furthermore, medicine, especially in powerful journeys, tends to cloud the mind. Memory and cognition are impaired (which is usually a good thing in such a setting), so the capacity to integrate insights and new states into our regular identity is more challenging, particularly without a guide's support. (However, in some cases, losing some of these faculties for a while can be very beneficial.)

Overall, it can be useful to familiarize yourself with and open yourself to these extra-conscious states prior to medicine work.

The Ability to Sense Energetic Phenomena in the Body

I thought I knew I had a body until my first MDMA journey. After 15 years of Dzogchen practice, windsurfing in my youth, karate, Krav Maga, ear surgeries, a broken arm, massages, and sex, I was confident I knew my body. I thought I knew what sensations in the body feel like. I did, but the bandwidth was narrow. Very narrow. I lived mostly from my neck up. I did not feel numb, I just did not know that my mind turned the volume down on sensing to a significant degree and for a very good reason: trauma.

Once the MDMA hit me in that first unforgettable journey, the emotion that initially came up was intense fear. I noticed I was too scared to go into my body and feel it. There was so much inside that I did not want to face. But the alternative of keeping on living life the way I had been felt so impossible now that going into my body was the only real choice. I understood at that moment that spirituality and Dzogchen had served me well, and I was grateful. But I had only taken the teachings part of the way. I had refused to allow awareness and attention to fully pervade my physical and psychic body and, therefore, used meditation and insights as a way to transcend reality in order to escape some of its aspects. I was living a half-life.

My guide asked for permission to put her hand on my chest, and she instantly became the mother I never had. I never doubted that my biological mother loved me deeply. But given her trauma and history, she could not really express it to me in my childhood. Once my body received permission with the help of the medicine to open itself to that loving hand, it began to drink.

The next insight was that love was absolutely surrounding me. I was swimming and breathing love through the main organ of emotional sensation in my psychic body, the heart (i.e., the heart chakra or heart center). I discovered that my heart was blocked from sensing and my heart chakra was closed. This insight led immediately to an opening of my heart chakra that I cannot describe in words. The best I can do is describe a somatic sensation of a beautiful flower that opens up when the sun shines on it. It is felt in the body. It is an energetic movement but absolutely sensed almost as a physical opening. Suddenly, you can breathe again and realize you have been holding your breath for years! In its fullest and most open expression, your heart, yourself, will love unconditionally anything and everything that manifests in consciousness. It will also love consciousness itself, yourself.

This process of energetic opening continued for several journeys and continues today with the opening and flexing of meridians and chakras. In addition, my sensitivity to energetic sensations has increased dramatically over time both with regard to my own sensation and the sensing of others physically nearby.

Having now seen many others going through similar experiences, I can say that I was ripe. Not because I was special or had a unique ability to perceive energetic phenomena (e.g., blocks in the system, the release of such blocks, energetic expansion, auras, and so on), but because I had done previous work in the energetic domain, I was a fertile ground for integrating novel somatic experience with an existing conceptual framework and a strengthened energy system.

The foundation I built, mostly unconsciously and without direct intent for a process that unfolded later in my life, included the following:

Reading and learning about the energy body—At age thirteen, I picked up my first book about chakras. I have no idea why or how it even got to my secular home in Israel. I recommend several books on this subject at the resources section.

Hatha yoga—I got into this practice while living in Nepal, where I spent six months in my early 20s. I believed that yoga was a form of exercise. My teacher was a young Nepalese male. When I asked him why he studied yoga, he told me it was because it cured his depression. I thought at the time that it was the strangest thing in the world because yoga was obviously just about the body. Little did I know.

Visualizations, meditations, and mantras—When I started practicing Dzogchen, I was introduced to visualizations of moving energy in the body, receiving energetic transmissions from teachers, reciting mantras to move energy in the body, and more.

In summary, I do not think that it is necessary to complete all of the above for a significant amount of time. However, I do believe that using some if not all of the above pathways for any duration of time can help people discover their energy system and have some familiarity with it before they begin working with medicine. At the very least, having common lingo with a guide who can explain and direct attention when appropriate in a journey will make the individual's journey more accessible and the work easier for the medicine teacher.

The Ability to Work with Resistance

Sooner or later, we will meet resistance in a journey or meditation. As discussed in the chapter "Ego," resistance is a normal part of the function of the ego and occurs regularly. On the mat, a guide can assist us with working with resistance. However, it is our responsibility to meet the medicine, the guide, and the teacher with an attitude and, potentially, a skillset that facilitates this process.

We can spend a long time in medicine journeys working with resistance instead of getting to the juicy stuff, such as communing with the divine, receiving teaching, experiencing alternate states of consciousness, and so on. Spending time with resistance is not a problem but rather a good thing, as resistance in a journey is an amplification of the subtle resistance we experience in life, one of the primary reasons for our daily sense of suffering.

Working with resistance is crucial to enlightenment. One can think about enlightenment and awakening as progression in defusing processes rather than finding something new or achieving a new state of being. In that sense, the work with resistance defuses subconscious processes that we ultimately experience as that resistance.

These subconscious processes of resistance are, in some ways, a major component of the glue that appears to bind consciousness and ego together. Once these loosen up, it is easier to notice the apparent gap between the two. Moreover, you notice that the ego, body, and all phenomena exist within consciousness and that you are the only knowing authority gazing out of your eyes.

The cherry on top is that when resistance relaxes, it hurts a lot less. There is less relative suffering and more flow with life. In a journey, this translates into reduced pain and increased efficacy and adaptability of the spirit medicine for any serious journeyer. Mushrooms would much rather teach you through play than rip off and compost layers and layers of energetic walls and cemented beliefs.

Here are two primary pointers regarding working with resistance.

INCREASE SENSITIVITY

Building the foundation for working with resistance requires becoming familiar with the somatic experience of that resistance. The somatic experience is unique to each person but generally involves a contraction in the body and the energy field and may include a deep sense of dread. It is important to increase the ability to detect resistance as early as possible. Most people who have never attended therapy or engaged in some sort of self-development process have no concept of resistance. They need to be conceptually educated first.

Psychoeducation about resistance helps people better understand what is happening to them during journeys rather than internalizing and identifying with their resistance (e.g., "I never launch; there's something wrong with me.").

During journeys and deep meditative experiences, several forms of resistance can occur. The leading cause is usually fear, whose depths are underestimated. All journeyers are aware of some nervousness, but they might not know the extent of their fear.

1. Intense mind movements—Thoughts come up rapidly and are very sticky, pulling the individual in multiple directions. This is a distraction and consists of ego protection in the dimensions of the head. The message is "Don't be clear. Remain confused." To counter that, working with the feet, directing energy to the legs, or placing a hand on the heart chakra can all be powerful in reducing the tendency to remain stuck in the head.

2. Failure to launch—The individual took the medicine and is lying there, waiting . . . but nothing is happening. There is no experience, just endless blackness staring back at them with absolute boredom. This is also possible in some meditations. It can be caused by an interference in the dimension of the head. Redirecting attention to somatic sensation and gentle bodywork can be very helpful. In addition, working with aromatic oils or other scents can trigger and amplify the experience.

3. Intense rigidity—This usually shows up as muscle rigidity (e.g., individuals lying very still and not moving, aching jaw, stiff neck, lack of mobility in the legs and pelvis) or as energetic rigidity, where the energy does not flow in the body. There is a sense of extreme heaviness in the individual, and sometimes it can extend

to the entire room. Assisting the individual to relax and calm down is beneficial. A gentle hand on the heart, slow breathwork, and music that promotes relaxing states are appropriate here.

Following psychoeducation, effort should be directed at increasing sensitivity in the ability to notice the content of thoughts as they arise (developed with open-awareness meditation) and the ability to sense changes in the psychic body (by engaging in meditation such as body scans, breathwork, chakra and energy visualizations, and so on). Medicine journeys will also be very powerful in increasing sensitivity to the psychic body if the intention is set.

RELAX

The most important aspect of working with resistance is learning to relax. While resistance is a contraction in the mind and body, relaxation is the opposite movement. Relaxation is a somatic sensation and ability. It is easier to teach relaxation at the level of the mind by teaching the mind to follow the body.

Make a fist. That is contraction. Now let go of the fist and let your arm fall loosely. That is relaxation. Learn to do this with your butt, chest, arms, legs, neck, belly, face, stomach, pelvic floor, feet, and so forth. Do it repeatedly until you become more and more familiar with the movement of relaxation.

One method I find very beneficial in helping clients become more familiar with resistance and diffusing it is the Wim Hof Method.

The Wim Hof Method is a way to keep your body and mind in its optimal natural state. I use two components of this method with clients: breathwork and cold exposure. Intense breathwork induces discomfort in the body, and sometimes pain, an energetic amplification that highlights blocks in the psychic body, hyperventilation, and sometimes anxiety. However, as opposed to medicine work, the individual has their foot on the gas pedal and can *decide* when to take it off. The method also incorporates phases of deep relaxation and states of bliss that contrast with the more active and triggering phases.

This process enables the individual to become more familiar with what it feels like when discomfort and contractions show up in the body, as the mind says, "No! I don't want to experience this!" Over time, this familiarity becomes more sensitive, and you can learn to redirect the mind and body to relax, just like you would relax a closed fist.

The second component I like to integrate from Wim Hof is cold exposure. There are few people who enjoy a cold shower first thing in the morning. When you stand in a hot shower and consider turning it to cold, there is often a moment of hesitation, a bracing in the body. That is resistance. Learn to sense it. Learn to breathe into it and relax the gross and then minute muscles that contract in anticipation. As the cold water hits your scalp and body, breathe. Learn how to work with breathing through pain, discomfort, and the nagging thought of *Why am I doing this?!*

Once clients are better able to meet resistance and have the ability to sustain three to four rounds of Wim Hof breathwork, I often like to introduce deeper and more intensive breathwork sessions. These usually last for about 45 to 60 minutes. These sessions are often a derivative adaptation of holotropic breathwork (developed by Christina and Stanislav Grof). Such breathwork is much more intense than Wim Hof. It amplifies energy in the psychic body on a larger scale and sometimes leads to full-blown psychedelic experiences. It could work as a replacement for medicine work when an individual is unable to engage with such medicine because of resistance, medical needs, or cultural causes. I highly recommend experimenting with this first on yourself with the help of a guide before attempting to engage others with this method. There are multiple holotropic breathwork trainings and workshops held internationally every year.

Whether one is evolving with meditation or medicine work, the skills outlined in this chapter are all crucial foundations for deep work. More specifically, the ability to work with our thoughts, feelings, attention, energy, identity, and resistance correlates to the rhythm and depth achievable in deep explorations into consciousness. We'll now focus on the use of psychedelic medicine in deep work, or more specifically, how the above-mentioned skills can be utilized and amplified by the benefits of psychedelics in therapeutic settings and the risks that these tools entail.

CHAPTER 6

MEDICINE

THIS CHAPTER IS NOT ORIENTED TOWARD TEACHING YOU HOW TO WORK
with medicine. I advise anyone who is interested in using medicine
for their own work or in working with others to seek mentors and teachers who can accompany them on this path. There are many traditions and
medicines. You will have to find the right one for you, probably through
experimentation. One primary piece of advice I can offer regarding working with medicine is that the focus is on building a deeper relationship with
yourself and with the medicine as a teacher. That means medicine work is
about learning to trust and listen, to give and receive.

Just as there was for me, there will probably be a period of trial and
error until you find an approach that works for you, and even then, life
will keep on shifting. I want to emphasize the importance of personal
experience. Please do not believe a doctrine or an approach without
authenticating it through your subjective experience. There is no objective
reality. There is no one path or one person who knows the entire spectrum
of the truth. You will have to seek and find it for yourself.

What Can Medicine Do?

I came out of my office into the waiting room at 4 p.m. to greet David as
usual and let him into the room. He got up from his seat and came straight
for a hug. This was unusual, as David previously presented as very stiff and
had a "don't come closer" biofield to him. However, the previous week, he
had a big opening in an MDMA journey with his guide, and he was finally
able to become intimate with his feelings, inner child, and consciousness.
As he had the somatic experience of being more intimate with himself, he
increased his capacity to be much closer to others.

He said as he sat down, "You know, our sessions before the journey were powerful, and I got a lot out of them, but they were like cracks in a concrete pavement. Our previous work did not penetrate me very much, even though I could see where it was going. The journey, on the other hand, was like a powerful pressure washer that completely broke the concrete away."

And so it is. Our self-development practices, therapy, and inner work are crucial in preparing the ground and psyche for a powerful transformation. Otherwise, using psychedelic medicine is like pouring enormous amounts of water on a concrete slab. The water, as powerful as it is, spills over the slab and cleans its surface but can't penetrate deep and remove the walls of our psyche. Once the cracks begin to form through our preparation for deep work, the water can find a way in and remove the toughest walls we did not even know were there.

One of my first psychedelic experiences was one of the most profound awakening states I have ever had.

At 26 years old, I was studying at Leiden University for a master's degree in clinical psychology. I was freshly divorced, as the relationship I had with my Dutch wife spontaneously dissolved when life pulled us in very different directions. Initially, I was terrified of the change. At that time in my life, I did not do well with change. But to my surprise, I found myself blossoming and rediscovering myself. My new American girlfriend, with whom I fell helplessly in love, introduced me to psilocybin mushrooms. Until that day, I had very little experience with substances. I was quite familiar with alcohol and had dabbled with cannabis in social settings but never felt compelled to use substances. I did not see the benefit of mind-altering drugs and did not like the feeling of loss of control in alternate states of consciousness. Little did I know that my hesitation with substances was an indication of what was buried in my psyche.

One day, while walking down a street in Amsterdam, Lindsey (my American girlfriend, who is now my wife and the mother of my children), Sabina (a sweet Mexican friend working on her PhD in anthropology and specializing in the Tarahumara tribe, whose members use hallucinogens to expand consciousness and develop spiritually), and I passed by a smart shop. At the time, psychedelics were legal in the Netherlands, and you could purchase them, similarly to cannabis, in what were called smart shops. I had absolutely no idea what I was getting into but trusted that an American from the San Francisco Bay Area and a Mexican anthropologist could show me the power of entheogenic plants.

The girls got very excited going through the shop menu, and we quickly left with a bunch of mushrooms in a bag. A few days later, we gathered in my bedroom to begin the experience. Lindsey and I had just finished a huge fight, which was a daily occurrence at the time. Both of us were young and needed repeated blows to our egos to transition into the next phase of life. We were somehow glad to give them to one another. Until that point in life, I had never had any issues with anger, but god almighty, could we bring it out in each other.

With zero preparation and absolutely no idea how much to take, I followed their lead, trusting they knew what they were doing.

After several years of meditation practice in the Dzogchen tradition, and in my hubris, I believed I had already come very close to seeing the nature of reality. Even though I had gone deep in my meditative experiences, I did not know how deep the rabbit hole goes. This time, the mushrooms were not taken in the frame of a spiritual or psychotherapeutic journey. It was a fun, recreational day filled with laughter and music with people I loved. Once the experience fully hit me, I was unprepared for the depths of consciousness I was about to explore.

There were two big highlights from that day that have stayed with me until today. The first was an embodied vision. I found myself to be an ancient yet ageless being sitting on a throne in a massively infinite dodecahedron. The walls were made out of hexagons. Each hexagon was an entire world, an entire life. I came into this vision by zooming out of a particular hexagon and realized that "my life," "my world," was only one of these hexagons. I became fully aware that I was living infinitely multiple lives simultaneously and was simply hypnotized by totally identifying with only one of these. I had focused on one world and forgot for "a brief moment" that I was living in them all at once. Zooming out of my life, I became this ageless being, hysterically laughing on the throne, touching for a brief moment the magnitude of life and god.

Coming down off the medicine, the second highlight manifested as boundless love pouring out of my heart. At this time in life, I knew about chakras and energy to some degree but had no conscious experience of energetic phenomena in my body. The three of us sat there, processing our experiences, and I was full of love for Lindsey, Sabina, myself, and the world. I was surprised, as this state of deep love was unfamiliar to me. It was a sharp contrast to the deep anger I had felt earlier in the day, and I could not find this love's source. It was refreshing, powerful, and life-altering.

Spiritual expansion is eventually seeing something that was always there. It depends on a perceptual shift. Nothing in our life circumstances actually changes. It is like looking at a tree through your living room window. Initially, you are focused on the tree outside (which is like the out-side world we experience), then after some time, you might see your own reflection in the window and become self-conscious (recognizing and then identifying with "me"). Then, with careful observation, you might notice the window itself, the surface of the window, as an entity of its own. This is like becoming aware of awareness itself, something that has always been there but was not noticed before. Lastly, in full integration, you might be able to perceive, feel, and embody the tree, your self-image, and the window all as one experience. The life story in the hexagon does not change one bit, but the perspective and identification change completely.

This perceptual shift can happen via meditation, an entheogenic journey, or a simple walk in the park. There is no one right way. Every person takes a different path, and their progress is individual and unduplicable. There is no one single algorithm that can work for all. Even structured spiritual approaches, such as Dzogchen or nondual Shaiva tantra, will manifest very differently for different people.

Therefore, working with a teacher and a guide is crucial to this process. A spiritual teacher has walked the path and has been through some of the pitfalls you are likely to encounter. They might not know the whole path, but they have enough insight to support you in your development. They can prescribe different practices, scriptures, and pointers that will be beneficial for you but perhaps not for someone else.

Similarly, when working with medicine, a guide has done work, established deeper relationships with entheogenic teachers, and seen more than you may have on that path. They can recommend using different entheogens for different purposes and recognize the dangers and pitfalls. More than that, a good guide will know when they have reached their limit and send you off to the next teacher.

How Psychedelics Work

This chapter does not cover the neurological and physiological aspects of entheogens. I encourage you to read scientific papers and books on this subject. It is currently a very popular field of study throughout the world, and new articles are coming out on a daily basis.

VEHICLES TO THE UNCONSCIOUS

Grossly, I divide psychedelics into synthetic versus organic compounds. The synthetic group includes substances such as MDMA, LSD, 5-MeO-DMT (when synthesized), 2C-B, and ketamine. The organic group includes entheogens such as cannabis, mushrooms (psilocybin), ayahuasca (DMT), mescaline (nonsynthesized), salvia, and more. The synthetic group works, in my experience, like a key that removes the veil between consciousness and the unconscious. Different substances unlock different depths and dimensions of consciousness. The organic group functions largely as nonhuman teachers or guides that have the power to take you by the hand and propel you through the veil to dimensions of consciousness that the spirits of the medicines guide you to see. In addition, these spirit teachers have multiple "powers" and agendas about which we know very little. Some of these powers include energetic cleansing, opening of blocks in the energy body, healing physical tissues, channeling beings from other dimensions, connecting us to our ancestors, and more. Their agendas could be anything from teaching us about the nature of reality, being messengers of love, and representing earth as an entity to propagation (i.e., mushrooms love to spread).

It is important to know that synthetic substances can be as important as organic entheogens. Some of the superpowers that entheogens have can also manifest in synthetic psychedelic experiences. However, they appear to happen without the presence of a guiding spirit and seem to be guided more by consciousness itself, our own inner teacher and healer.

ENERGETIC MANIPULATION

All substances, but especially psychedelics, are amplifiers of energy and inner phenomena. These substances infuse the psychic body with intense amounts of energy. Individuals who have had these experiences often describe feeling enormous currents of energy flowing through their body. This could be sensed in the chakras, meridians, organs, and extremities. The sensation could feel like "fire was coming out of my head and butt at the same time," as a client told me once after having a ketamine experience with their guide.

The increase in energetic input to our body via these substances highlights the blocks, samskaras, and degree of openness of our chakras. As these are highlighted, we can become more aware of the condition of our psychic body and then work with it appropriately. In a journey, when energy lines and centers are highlighted, the client and guide have the opportunity to facilitate release via various modalities, such as bodywork, redirection, breathwork, and extraction.

The Pitfalls and Risks of Working with Medicine

1. *Psychological dependency*—One of the biggest pitfalls of doing medicine work is developing a spiritual or psychological reliance on medicine to achieve deep states of meditation. For many, learning how to meditate and enter deep states of consciousness can be a frustrating process that, at times, particularly without proper guidance, can last years. Medicine can accelerate this process by giving us a taste or glimpse of what lies beyond the horizon. It is easier to remember the taste of chocolate once you've had it rather than seek an experience only described to you. However, the risk

is that, if we taste an alternate state of consciousness with the help of medicine, we begin a process of conditioning: "I can arrive at this place only with the help of medicine. I do not have this state within me or the skills I need to arrive at this place." In addition, the medicine colors the alternate state of consciousness achieved somatically, emotionally, and cognitively. Therefore, when using medicine to achieve higher states of consciousness, the following are crucial in my opinion:

    a. Follow expansive states of consciousness achieved with medicine with sober meditation practice.

    b. In sober meditation practice, notice the differences between expansive states of consciousness under the influence of medicine and without. For example, under the influence of mushrooms (i.e., psilocybin), consciousness can feel twisted, loving, folded, and so on. That is not the default state of human consciousness but is like the mushroom's state of consciousness. Ultimately, it is important to notice that all content appearing in consciousness (including thoughts, feelings, and somatic perceptions) is an apparition and does not define consciousness or the experiencer.

2. *New identification*—One of the main issues with the use of psychedelics is that they open us to a new field of experience. This range of possibilities is unlimited: meeting the divine, witnessing creation itself, out-of-body experiences, healing, talking to aliens, communicating with animals, communicating with the spirit of the medicine, and so on and so forth. Due to the ego and its power of appropriation, these new experiences can be easily incorporated into a new identity set: "Now I have evolved. I have seen creation. I have changed into a new person." The content of the psychedelic experience becomes a part of the content of the mind, hypnotizing the subject and reinforcing the "me" story. This is not necessarily a problem and possibly just a step

in the right direction for spiritual evolution. However, if one is interested in complete spiritual expansion, in finding out the deepest core of reality, this fascination with inner content is not different from a fascination with money, cars, or body image; it will slow one down in the search for spiritual enlightenment. Furthermore, as the ego now has access to new material it can incorporate into its identity, it will expand its adventure of self-improvement. Clients can spend many years discovering hidden parts and unresolved emotions, and when one finishes processing one's trauma from their current life, past life patterns begin to emerge. Samsara is infinite. The goal of self-improvement is ever-elusive and does not end. This does not mean that the process is useless but that at some point, even inner exploration needs to be seen through, and the ego itself, as a vehicle, needs to be examined and seen for what it is: not our essence or true identity.

3. *Physical harm*—In general and physiologically speaking, most psychedelics are some of the safest substances one can consume. However, there are some medicines that have a higher risk profile. For example, MDMA can elevate blood pressure and pulse and is, therefore, dangerous for individuals with untreated blood pressure, a history of stroke, or heart conditions. In addition, MDMA is not appropriate for people taking SSRIs due to the risks of overflooding the brain with serotonin (i.e., serotonin syndrome). Ibogaine is a very powerful psychedelic that can complicate heart problems, seizures, and liver toxicity. In summary, it is crucial to have a guide who understands the risks, dosages, and appropriateness of psychedelic medicines when working with others.

4. *Psychological stress*—Psychedelic journeys, like hiking the Himalayas, often have a little bit of everything: beauty, love, and wholeness, but also pain, suffering, anger, and fear. The entire spectrum of human experience is available to us and likely to be

triggered sooner or later in our journeys. Moreover, repressed content and samskaras are bound to rise to the surface. Contrary to common beliefs, a "bad" trip is not bad. It is positive for our development, as it forces us to face and digest potent and substantial samskaras, deep maladaptive beliefs (e.g., I exist as a separate entity), or a powerful self-image (e.g., "I am the best" or "I am worthless"). However, there are times in life when we are psychologically and physically more fragile and can be easily overwhelmed by medicine. For example, consider not journeying if you are physically sick. The toll on your body can be significant and recovery lengthy. In contrast, sometimes mushrooms, peyote, or ayahuasca are appropriate for people seeking healing and a cure for cancer, arthritis, autoimmune disorders, and other medical conditions. The role of a guide is irreplaceable in such conditions. Additionally, some psychological states are riskier than others when working with medicine, such as schizophrenia, bipolar disorder, and personality disorders. Each one has its own complications and is not an immediate no. I have witnessed the suffering of people with bipolar or schizophrenia having to take psychotropic medications that numb their body and soul. I wish for them to be healed, and medicine could be a healing aid in some cases. However, journeying in a private residence without proper staff and support can be dangerous in such situations for both journeyer and guide.

DIFFICULT JOURNEYS

I would like to share a few examples of difficult journeys and the lessons they help teach us about the proper use of these medicines.

James was a rigid man in his 50s, a software engineer with a mild case of OCD who had never tried psychedelics. Contemporary psychotherapy over the course of ten years yielded some but very limited results. He began working with a guide and had several MDMA journeys over the course of a year, which opened his heart and enabled him to feel deeply connected to himself and others. Following his personal work, he was invited to a medicine group journey. Group journeys are often more potent, as the energy of the group tends to amplify the strength of the medicine, and repressed content is more likely to arise. This was an MDMA group journey, which tends to be more peaceful in nature. However, during the journey, James reported that a "dark entity" showed up in his mind and began to torment him.

This began a process of psychological decompression that required close work with several of the guides present that night. James experienced an intense somatic and psychological release in the days following the journey, which helped him to integrate his experiences from the journey into his psychology. Ultimately, he became aware that the dark entity was an archetypal and previously unconscious presentation of his abusive and strict father, who was also a pastor. Had James not received support both during and after the journey, he could have easily externalized the dark entity into a "demon" and created an entire new narrative about it that would have further complicated his inner world.

Sara was a wise and very experienced guide in the medicine community. Yet, in her early days of medicine work, she was encouraged to try 5-MeO-DMT, probably prematurely. 5-MeO-DMT can produce a wide range of phenomena but, in adequate dosages, often leads to a complete ego dissolution: "You simply dissolve into nothingness and merge into the universe." For the uninitiated, this can be overwhelming and frightening. I personally tried 5-MeO-DMT following years of meditative and medicine experiences, including "ego dissolution," and still categorize my experience on 5-MeO-DMT as the most intense psychedelic experience I have ever had. It is absolutely not for the fainthearted. For Sara, the intensity of the experience was so overwhelming, frightening, and disorienting that she did not "land" (i.e., come back to herself) for many weeks following this experience. In the long term, it was beneficial, and today she works with this medicine with herself and others but is wise in her administration and choice of when and how to use it.

Toby, a woman in her 40s who suffered from severe anxiety, took months to prepare for an MDMA journey. Her guide was confident that her first journey would, at the very least, give her a taste of freedom, of what life can feel like without anxiety, given that the amygdala (i.e., the alarm center of the brain) tends to shut down under the medicine's influence. However, twenty minutes after ingestion, Toby locked down in a panic attack that lasted four hours, despite all the guide's attempts to help her surrender to the experience. She described those hours as some of the worst moments of her life. Like Sara, Toby's experience helped her in the long term to release intense fear in her body, which was always present underneath the surface. Yet, during the journey and in the weeks following the experience, she required support, guidance, and tender, loving care to help her navigate that experience.

In summary, we do not know how the ego will react to psychedelic experiences. The ego is vast, complex, and has its self-preservation instincts. Always work with an experienced guide who has walked the path before you. This is not just about certification or coursework. I know many certified psychologists and guides who have very little experience or courage to shine the light of awareness deep into their being. Be wise in your choices.

The Medicines: Our Nonhuman Teachers

Before describing the use of some of the medicines below, a couple of notes: despite my love and appreciation for medicine, my familiarity with psychedelics is limited to certain medicines, including cannabis, MDMA, psilocybin, ketamine, and 5-MeO-DMT. My personal use of these medicines has been for consciousness expansion and working with trauma and the samskaras held in my body. My discussion of these medicines will be limited to these areas.

Discussion of dosage is beyond the scope of this book. In addition, I personally do not believe that there is an algorithm that can give an accurate dose chart for different psychedelic medicines. Dosages depend on intention, user sensitivity (their level of permeability to experience), purpose of use, tolerance, pharmaceuticals in their bloodstream, resistance, and so on. A general rule of thumb is that the higher the dose, the stronger the potential for the effects described below. However, for each substance, there will be a point of threshold after which the nervous system and body will become overwhelmed and a sense of overdose could occur. Overdose does not necessarily result in death, but it can result in vomiting, numbness, and intense psychological distress.

There are always caveats to the effects described below, as people may react in unexpected ways to these substances.

CANNABIS (I.E., MARIJUANA, GRASS, POT, WEED)

Weed was present in my life in Israel from early childhood. It is very popular in the Middle East and usually used recreationally. In my youth in Israel, it was mostly illegally imported from Bedouin tribes in the Sinai Peninsula as dry branches with flowers full of seeds (not a good sign, as users usually prefer to smoke female plants without the seeds they develop once pollinated by male plants). The other popular form of marijuana in Israel, which was easier to smuggle into the county, was hashish, a brown or black tar made by distilling the marijuana flowers into a paste that hardens over time. As marijuana can usually be expensive, it is often mixed with tobacco in most parts of the world. Either the flower is ground with tobacco or pieces of hashish are integrated into the tobacco and rolled into a spliff. This works well, as tobacco smoking was and still is very common in Israeli society.

My father introduced marijuana to my brother and sister as I was growing up. I was never particularly interested, though I tried it once prior to joining the IDF shortly after my 18th birthday. I did not feel an effect after taking my first hit and stayed away from marijuana until my early 20s. As my friends got discharged from the IDF, they began backpacking around the world (most Israelis go backpacking in South America and Asia following their release from the military). They came back and brought the habit of smoking marijuana with them. Every Friday night, we would get together in the basement of a close friend's house and spend hours smoking and passing a bong into the early morning. It was fun, purely recreational, and a way for a group of young men to connect emotionally. However, I still did not like it much. I found that it often made me feel anxious and out of control. This was also true of another friend who grew up in a dysfunctional family. Friends who came from more stable backgrounds seemed to be doing great and could keep on smoking with no apparent limit.

I eventually left Israel and moved to Europe, following my Dutch girlfriend and pursuing another way of life. Despite spending a great deal of time in Amsterdam (which was, at the time, one of the only places in the world where marijuana was decriminalized and easily accessible), I never thought of marijuana or came close to it. The only time I would consume it was when my Israeli friends would come and visit.

In 2010, I moved to San Francisco. Even then, although I had access to marijuana and mushrooms, it never came into my life. If I found myself in social situations where it was offered, I might have taken a puff or two, but it did not stick to me at all.

In March 2013, I became a father to my son Adi. It was the most beautiful and overwhelming experience of my life. A few months into the experience of parenthood, marijuana found its way into my life. No one pushed me or introduced me to it. I just woke up one day and wanted to smoke. It was lovely. It was medicine. It relaxed my body. It allowed me to turn my mind off at the end of the day after caring for him. I did, however, have to be careful not to use too much of it, as it made me anxious at times. I was an occasional user, only in the evenings and mostly on the weekends. About six months into this occasional habit, I had my first panic attack on marijuana.

Little did I know that the spirit of the plant was slowly working its way through the rigid walls that kept my unconscious at bay. My childhood trauma was making its way out, triggered by becoming a father, and marijuana was there to help it along. One evening, I took one puff too many with the wrong crowd. A few minutes later, I became certain that I was going to die. A tremendous sense of terror took hold of my guts and heart, and my entire world imploded in upon itself. The worst part of it all was that, as a young psychologist in training, I knew exactly what was happening to me, but I could not stop it. Only Lindsey's gentle, loving touch, her reassurance that she was with me, helped bring the incident to a conclusion.

I was safe enough to let the waves of energetic release wash over me. It was my unintended first medicine journey.

That scared the living shit out of me, and I stayed away for a few years. However, in 2018, my daughter Alma was born, and being parents of a young baby took its toll on both of us. Now in San Diego, without family support, I turned to marijuana again, but I was careful. This time, I became habituated and learned how to be a stoner. By the time COVID hit at the beginning of 2020, I was a daily user and was caught in a cycle of addiction. Marijuana became a mistress, a teacher, and a powerful spirit. She had a lot to teach me despite my sincere attempts to break away.

My personal relationship with marijuana is a classic example of how a relationship with a medicine spirit can become very complicated.

With marijuana, it's important to remember that, despite the legalization and popularization of the plant in the western hemisphere in the last few years, there is still a lot that we do not know or understand about its biomechanics. A close friend, who is a leading biological chemist and researcher in the Netherlands, once told me that, although we have identified THC and CBD as the main active ingredients in the plant, there are hundreds of other molecules that play an integral role in the mechanism of action. Research is ongoing, but we simply do not understand the entirety of how marijuana works. In addition, from a personal and spiritual perspective, marijuana is a living spirit and a nonhuman teacher. It works in other dimensions beyond the regular physical, biochemical pathways that we can see and measure.

To simplify this discussion, I will focus on CBD and THC. There are many different strains of marijuana, and growers around the world develop more each day. The trend is to increase the percentage of active ingredients to create a more powerful experience for users. This is, unfortunately, both unnecessary and potentially dangerous, but the market has a life of its own. CBD is often perceived to have anti-inflammatory effects, decreasing pain, and does not cause perceptual shifts. THC is commonly perceived as the molecule that induces the sought-after "high" and is also connected with increased anxiety and perceptual shifts.

Nevertheless, marijuana has many gifts:

1. *Physiological*—It can calm the body, reduce inflammation, and decrease pain, especially when using strains that contain high percentages of CBD. In addition, despite the "munchies" that many marijuana users experience, it turns out that regular use of the plant tends to regulate sugar levels in the blood. Many diabetics (both type 1 and 2) regularly use marijuana to regulate sugar levels and prevent hypo and hyperglycemia.

2. *Sexual*—Marijuana is an erotic spirit. It usually increases sexual arousal and improves sexual encounters. Whether this is due to increased blood flow or reduced inhibition is unknown. However, if one wants to work on improving their sex life or using sex as a spiritual practice to become more intimate with the divine, marijuana can be of assistance.

3. *Energetic*—Marijuana is an amplifier of energy in the psychic body. If there is anything stuck, if there is a samskara ready to be looked at or experienced, marijuana will highlight it and prepare it for digestion, providing a conscious experience of it. This is often experienced as strong sensations in the body, areas of pain, pressure, or movement. In my opinion, this is the leading cause of increased anxiety, spiraling down into negative thought patterns and panic attacks. Most people who experience such symptoms try to avoid these experiences via distraction (e.g., watching movies, focusing on interpersonal interaction), increasing the dose (disabling the mechanism of the experience and inducing numbness), or taking other medications that reduce anxiety (e.g., Xanax). It will be much more beneficial to work with a guide if possible or, if alone, with the intention to allow oneself to surrender to the somatic experience and allow full digestion of samskaras. Negative thought spirals, for example, are usually an indication of energy stuck in the head region.

4. *Insights*—Marijuana is a teacher. She can give direct teachings regarding the nature of reality and the world of plants (as she is a plant spirit) or she can function as a bridge to other teachers and realities, piercing the veil and allowing teachings and insights to come into our mind.

Such insights could be in words, thoughts, visions, or somatic experiences (e.g., "I know it in my bones.").

5. *Integration*—As will be further discussed in the following chapter, marijuana is a wonderful aid in the process of integration and embodiment. Marijuana can facilitate the transfer of insights in the form of thoughts into feelings and somatic experiences in the body.

The primary risk I see with marijuana is its potential for psychological addiction. However, when compared to psychological and physical addiction to alcohol, I do not think it poses a major risk to people's lives. I'd much rather live in a society of lazy stoners than angry drunks.

In addition, chronic use of marijuana can often result in depression, social isolation, and decreased motivation to do anything other than use marijuana. Managing one's relationship with this substance is not simple. If this medicine becomes your ally, do your best to take breaks and turn to help if you have lost control of this relationship.

MDMA (I.E., ECSTASY, MOLLY)

MDMA is often referred to as "heart medicine" in the psychedelic therapy community. When taken properly, with intention and adequate preparation and integration, it can perform miracles. It does not always work this way, but in most of the cases I've learned about, people who go through their first MDMA journey experience a significant shift. Huge shifts can happen. And at times, miracles. I really mean it.

MDMA is incredibly beneficial for all sorts of conditions, mild, moderate, and severe. Pain and suffering are all relative. So, MDMA can be very effective in working with depression, anxiety, and panic attacks but also chronic anxiety, severe trauma, and, in some cases, even personality disorders and psychosis. However, the set and setting are crucial, and the guide has to be highly skilled and specialize in working with these populations and mental health conditions.

As a psychologist, I have been blessed to sit with people in the depths of mental health crises. Vietnam vets, policemen, criminals, women who were raped repeatedly, people with personality disorders, 9/11 World Trade Center survivors, people who lost limbs to cancer, fathers who lost their children, mothers who lost their babies, partners who lost their spouses to suicide/cancer/an affair, refugees, and so many more.

To see someone with a narcissistic personality disorder say, "I know that I am full of myself. I do not know how to stop. Could you help me?" and then seeing them drop that entire character is like seeing your political nemesis become human. Now they can admit the falseness, the lies, the grandiosity, and the insatiable hunger for power. It is like seeing behind the curtain and meeting the actual soul for several hours, during which a real conversation can occur. In the end, they simply want to be loved and love back.

As a psychologist, it is magic! I could not believe it the first time I witnessed it. But again and again, this medicine has left me speechless.

Eduardo is a South American man who was raised in a cult deep in the Amazon. His parents were forced to get pregnant and bring him into the world. Growing up in the cult, he was severely physically, sexually, and emotionally abused. His parents neglected him and did not protect him. He and other children were bullied by adults and older peers. His father committed suicide. By the time he got to me, Eduardo was suffering from severe depression, a very painful case of IBS, and repeated, uncontrollable panic attacks. The SSRIs that he had been living on for years had stopped working, and he was now a chronic cannabis user, which helped him deal with the physical pain associated with IBS.

Previously, Eduardo had been diagnosed with schizophrenia due to psychotic symptoms that could arise when he was very badly depressed. His hallucinations and delusions were expectedly paranoid in nature: "Someone is coming after me." In truth, I believe his psychosis was an expression of several samskaras that were attempting to release. Someone did come after him as a child, but he could not face it or experience the entire event. Several samskaras were created then and there.

We worked on deep work foundations in therapy for several months and went quite far. There were some significant cracks in the concrete wall.

Eduardo now had access to several protectors and exiled parts. He had been able to come in contact with and release several samskaras. The Wim Hof Method and other exercises lifted the depression and panic attacks. He was ripe for work and responded beautifully. This was all without any medicine, except the cannabis that he was still using.

However, the IBS did not improve. It was still causing him a lot of pain, and he was smoking a lot of weed to cope, which had undesirable effects. Eduardo was also still suffering from several persistent pejorative thoughts: "You're a failure! You're a loser! I am going to get you!"

About three months into our work, Eduardo had his first MDMA journey with a guide whom I know very well, someone I trusted to have the skillset and courage necessary to work with someone with this level of trauma.

A week later, Eduardo was back in my office. His face was completely transformed. There was a sense of ease and contentment that I never knew was even missing. The grimace that had made his eyes squint, clenched his jaw, and contracted his brow was gone. His eyes were bigger, and the smile reached the corners of his eyes. It was like seeing a person reborn. At least that was the way he described it. There were two important takeaways from Eduardo's journey that he shared with me.

Shortly after the journey began, an external demon appeared in the form of a "dark black skeleton witch, and she wanted to eat me." Seeing a vision like this is unusual for MDMA sessions but not unheard of in cases of severe trauma. The guide conducted a very simple but firm cleansing/exorcism using flame, smoke, prayer, and feathering. This was culturally aligned with Eduardo, and he felt cleansed afterward. This event correlated to an immediate and sustained cessation of the thought movement "You're a failure! You're a loser! I am going to get you!"

The second important event was the discovery of the heart space: "I felt my heart chakra. I saw it completely imploded, and when I saw it, it responded to me. It woke up and started opening."

On the journey, the guide helped Eduardo to open his heart center with touch and energy work. As previously mentioned, experiencing the opening of the heart center is an awakening experience. There is no doubt left, if this is a conscious experience, that you still have love within you. That you are capable of feeling love, being loved, receiving love, and seeing the world from a loving perspective. When someone like Eduardo can see the world from love, even if only for several hours, it can feel like a concrete slab was lifted off their chest. Most of the time, they do not even feel the presence of the weight or understand how cumbersome it is. His thank you note to the guide said, "Thank you for giving me my life back."

The primary strengths of MDMA in my opinion are the following:

1. *Owl vision*—It allows a sense of clarity when examining issues. The answers come easily, feel genuine, and make sense. Beginner users tend to be hyperverbal while under the influence. There is cognitive and conceptual access to almost everything that wants to be examined. There is an ability to see through ego defenses and feel the emotion associated with the truth.

2. *Heart opening*—For whatever reason, energetic or biological, MDMA tends to open the heart chakra. Users often feel a sensation of openness, warmth, spaciousness, and deep relaxation in the chest. This is even more amplified when lying down on a comfortable mattress, preferably with covered eyes, in a journey space that is dark with appropriate accompanying music. The heart opening is often associated with deep and blissful waves of unconditional love that initially appear to come from deep within us but with increased attention and work will also be perceived as coming from all directions. This experience alone is psychologically and spiritually transformative, in my opinion. It sets a new bar for life. Even if that state is substance-induced, one comes to realize that there are ways we can orient ourselves toward such states that are different from the default state of life we used to know.

3. *Intense energetic amplification*—MDMA tends to blast the body with additional energy. Sold on the street, it is often cut with methamphetamines or other substances that create a speedy effect. Therefore, it is often used at parties and raves. The stuff that is used in psychotherapeutic settings is usually purer and less speedy, allowing the user to focus, in the right set and setting, on inner experience. The amplification of the energy in the body assists us in discovering unconscious samskaras, other energetic blockages, and narrowing of the meridians. These show up as specific sensations in locations in the body during and after journeys. Additional inquiry into these sensations and their locations often produces memories, insights, visions, emotional experiences, or thought streams that have potentially therapeutic effects.

Prior to my own journey work, I tried MDMA in a recreational setting and had a nice experience connecting with my wife. But I had no idea of its therapeutic potential. Many of my clients who previously tried MDMA recreationally and then had guided MDMA sessions disclosed that they were "floored" by the depth and power of the medicine when used with intention, a guide, and in an appropriate set and setting.

NEGATIVE ASPECTS OF MDMA

The addiction potential of MDMA is low, in my opinion. The addicts that I know are predominantly individuals who use a lot of molly to party. Their lives could be characterized as going from one party to another. These are often highly social individuals going through a certain phase of life associated with diminished boundaries (e.g., sexual promiscuity, being in between jobs, prolific substance abuse) but also openness to meditation, yoga, spirituality, and personal work. Other frequent users of MDMA are individuals who use it to release and relax on a weekly basis from the extremely stressful positions that they find themselves in life. These are know-it-all control freaks who do everything and struggle to delegate. I am not very concerned about addiction to MDMA, especially when it is taken in therapeutic or ceremonial settings. In addition, the price that your body will pay (in terms of exhaustion afterward) is relatively high and often discourages users from frequent, repeated experiences.

The biggest issue I have with MDMA is the toll it takes on the body. This differs from one person to another. In general, during the journey, there is usually an increase in heart rate, dehydration, and elevated body temperature. This is usually not felt consciously and not a problem, but it can be dangerous for people with heart conditions, untreated high blood pressure, or other illnesses (e.g., autoimmune disorders, cancer, and so on). Therefore, working with MDMA with vulnerable individuals requires great caution and consideration.

Furthermore, there could be side effects following the journey. Many people only need a good night's sleep, but some experience significant mood swings in the week following the journey. Some experience vertigo or significant fatigue and need several days to recover. I personally feel very fatigued and drained for about a week following an MDMA journey.

There are supplements one can take to counter some of these effects, but there is no established data yet on whether this is just another vitamin trend or if there is really a way to offset an MDMA hangover.

Overall, in my opinion, when comparing benefits to risks, doing an MDMA journey in a safe manner is very helpful and conducive to emotional and spiritual change, especially with people with significant histories of trauma.

KETAMINE

Ketamine was originally developed as an anesthetic drug in the '60s. It was used primarily in medical settings as a surgical anesthetic and for pain management and then extensively in the Vietnam War.

To the surprise of the medical staff in these settings, many patients treated with high dosages of ketamine returned from anesthesia disoriented and, at times, very agitated. They often came back to themselves asking, "Where the fuck was I?!" People had stories about disappearing but regaining consciousness in a black hole in which nothing happened (i.e., the infamous "k-hole"), meeting aliens or their ancestors, receiving teachings, experiencing unconditional love, witnessing the big bang or the creation of the cosmos, swimming with dolphins in the ocean, or other psychedelic experiences.

It turns out that ketamine is a dissociative substance. It allows the user to dissociate from the body and the ego and allows the unconscious to manifest to various degrees, depending on the dose administered.

Ketamine is currently approved by the FDA for use as an anesthetic and for treatment-resistant depression via a medical model. This is often done via a prescription of intranasal spray or IV administration in ketamine clinics. The effects of ketamine are usually short-lived, lasting only a few days to several weeks, but there does not seem to be much validation for the long-term effects of repeated use of ketamine.

The psychedelic therapy community generally does not adhere to the medical model utilizing ketamine. The main points of criticism of the standard medical model include lack of guidance during the experience, lack of a program for integration, and the fact that administrated dosages are often sub-psychedelic and do not allow for the conscious experience of extra-conscious states.

Eli, a male in his late 20s, suffered from treatment-resistant depression. He followed a six-week treatment protocol (once a week) in a ketamine clinic. This was not covered by insurance. In San Diego, it is $800 a pop. In every session, a kind nurse led him to a private room, connected him to an IV line, turned on the TV that displayed a calm video with accompanying euphoric music, and dimmed the lights. The anesthesiologist would sometimes check in on him, but after the first session, it was only the nurse who started the IV and then disappeared for 45 minutes, as she had other patients to check on. An hour later, Eli would rise from his experience, which he described as sleepy and euphoric, and was then driven home by his parents. During the six-week course, his depression lifted significantly. This was a big improvement, as Eli did not respond at all to psychotherapy or psychotropic medications.

However, two weeks after his last ketamine IV treatment, the depression came back, and Eli needed a monthly administration to keep him feeling better.

Ketamine is an unusual psychedelic because it works on a different set of receptors in the brain. Whereas psilocybin (i.e., mushrooms), DMT (i.e., ayahuasca), and mescaline (i.e., San Pedro and peyote) work primarily with serotonin receptors, ketamine works on NMDA receptors that involve the neurotransmitter glutamate. This causes a gradual shutting down of our senses, and the user can temporarily dissociate from their body and mind. When used in the psychedelic community, it is often administered as a lozenge or via insufflation (i.e., snorting) and generates a shorter one- to two-hour journey (compared to the five- to six-hour journey with MDMA or mushrooms), unless it is integrated with other medicine.

Although dissociation has a bad reputation, especially in the trauma community, the psychedelic therapy community sees great benefits of working with ketamine in the following cases:

1. Highly resistant individuals who are very fearful of turning inside often have extreme forms of anxiety and/or panic attacks, are very sober in their lives, and exert a great deal of control over themselves, their environment, and others. A gradual administration of ketamine to these individuals (especially using ketamine lozenges) can be very helpful as an introduction of alternate states of consciousness and temporality, shutting down the hypervigilant activation of the body.

2. As ketamine is medically relatively safe in small and medium doses, it is easier to work with among individuals who have medical conditions that disqualify them from working with MDMA.

3. Advanced journeyers who are ready to experience states of ego dissolution, commonly known as ego death, can really benefit from ketamine. The temporary experience of ego death can happen on a variety of medicines. However, it is more common with the use of 5-MeO-DMT and high dosages of ketamine. There will be more about the experience of ego death in the next chapter. Beyond the ego death experience, ketamine is also very powerful

in connecting us to higher realms in moderate to high dosages. I have personally had a very vivid conversation with my long-dead father, who came to me during a ketamine journey in body and spirit. It was a therapeutic experience that I will forever be grateful for. For advanced journeyers, the route of administration usually involves insufflation or intramuscular (IM) injections.

4. Ketamine is also a wonderful way to allow for the integration of mental insights (e.g., thoughts and feelings) and a deeper sense of knowing into somatic experiences. Ketamine can facilitate uninhibited dancing or bilateral body movements that cross the body's midline (an important facet of integration in psychotherapeutic approaches such as EMDR) and assist in other forms of psychological and somatic integration.

Ketamine has a higher risk for psychological addiction. A lot of people like to do K in a party setting. It can be a fun substance to dance on, as it facilitates dissociation, which reduces inhibition. Especially when snorted, it can be very potent and become psychedelic as well.

It is not uncommon to develop nausea during or after the use of ketamine. Some people just do not do very well with this medicine. Prior to use, most people should abstain from food for about four hours. Sometimes people cannot eat for several hours following a ketamine journey.

PSILOCYBIN

For me, mushrooms are the ultimate healers. As an imprinted control freak, they also used to terrify me.

There are many different types of psilocybin mushrooms, and my knowledge of them is limited. The commonly identified psychoactive compounds in mushrooms are psilocybin and its less-known colleague psilocin. Humans cannot directly utilize psilocybin in the nervous system, so the liver converts that molecule into psilocin, which is the actual active molecule that causes the magic mushrooms' psychedelic effects.

Mushrooms are considered to be earth medicine. Fungi are beings that specialize in connectivity (i.e., mycelium) and breaking down dead organisms. It is a medicine focused on the connectivity of all living beings to each other and to the earth from which we come. When I say earth, I mean the archetype of the earth. Mushrooms love Mother Earth as well (i.e., Pachamama), but the concept of earth means the ground that all creation comes from: love itself, god itself. While working with MDMA, a guide usually has more input on where the journey will go, but mushrooms are different. The mushrooms are center stage, and it is unpredictable where the journey can lead.

In an MDMA journey, there are three people in the room: the client, the guide, and the client's higher Self, which emerges when the medicine strips the ego down. In a mushroom journey, the spirits of the mushrooms enter the room. Although the mushrooms are technically dead and usually dried up when eaten, many guides see the ingestion as giving permission to the spirits to enter the body and direct our experience. Many individuals report that the journey actually begins a few days prior to ingestion. This manifests as unusual dreams, interpersonal conflicts, meditative experiences (including visions), and being hyperemotional.

I see two main areas where mushrooms like to do their work:

HEALING

The mushrooms are truly benevolent healers and very powerful in composting shadow material and samskaras, as well as in removing blockages from meridians and chakras. Sometimes, it almost feels to me like some kind of symbiosis is taking place. The mushrooms appear to thoroughly enjoy feeding on any stuck emotion or energy in our body, and in return, we get to liberate some very painful burdens in the process.

A day before one of my first guided mushroom journeys, I was sitting on a plane to San Francisco, traveling to see my guide the next day. As the plane took off into the sunset, I began to sob without reason. I had no idea why. The following day, as the mushrooms started to come on, the crying and sobbing returned, and I found myself on the bed remembering my many ear surgeries.

When I was sixteen years old, a tumor destroyed my left inner ear. In 1993, ENT surgeries in Israel were a butchery compared to those in San Diego in 2015. There were a series of very painful surgeries that required significant hospitalizations. Ear pain, which is really not fun at all, was present for a significant portion of my early and middle teens. I never realized that I was carrying that pain and fear in my body. I thought that my trick of turning away from the pain solved the problem, but it turns out I was just saving it for later.

The mushrooms showed me where and how I was holding pain and fear in my body. They also showed me the capacity for unconditional love that they had, that I had, and that nature had, and they allowed me to see and experience all the pain that my body had had to endure. The mushrooms then ate this samskara with me and released it from my body while showing me the entire process. It was beautiful, merciful, painful, and magical. Like giving birth. Following this release, I experienced going into spontaneous yoga positions that I had never learned. There was a compulsion to move my body in certain patterns that facilitated stretches and various yogic postures.

Mushrooms are also known to have detoxification effects and end addiction to substances, at least on a temporary basis. I know many people who stopped drinking alcohol and smoking weed or tobacco following a single journey with mushrooms. I have personally stopped drinking coffee and using marijuana for weeks or months on end following journeys with mushrooms. This is a big deal for me, as I have no interest in stopping drinking coffee and have been drinking two to three cups of it since my late teens. I just cannot take a look at or sometimes even smell coffee after a journey.

Many times, mushrooms also cause individuals to stay away from animal flesh for several weeks. This is, again, not something I generally do, as I am an avid carnivore and grew up on a meat-rich diet. However, many studies indicate that eating a plant-rich diet without meat for a time can be detoxifying and beneficial for our body and energy system.

TEACHERS

The mushrooms are great teachers of spiritual expansion. Their method of teaching is unusual. Certain lineages in Mexico see them as tricksters. They like to play games, and their world is twisted and folded on itself. Their favorite game is hide and seek, "come and find me." But more than anything, they like to play with the ego as a form of teaching.

They especially like resistance and will highlight all the ways you think you are not resisting them: "Oh, you're not scared. Then let me show you exactly how much and where in your body there are . . . " But despite their trickster nature, they are benevolent. If you come with a question or intention for the journey, you will very likely emerge with an answer that's probably a lot more than you asked for.

Working with the mushrooms can be very intense, physically, emotionally, and spiritually. They will take you all the way if needed. If ego death is desired or required, they are absolutely able to cross that line, although it is less common. Ego death or, more accurately in my opinion, ego pause is an experience wherein one's sense of identity is temporarily dissolved and can lead to profound redefining of the self.

The mushrooms can teach by showing alternate dimensions, providing experiences of unity consciousness, showing reality in other scales (e.g., geometric levels of reality, quantum levels of reality, and deeper layers of biology, even down to molecules), downloading instructions and material into our mind, and assisting in the processing of exploring existential topics such as life and death, space and time, killing and being killed.

Personally, I have had very significant spiritual experiences assisted by mushrooms. These included seeing the dynamism of creation and how energy becomes matter, having an audience with the angel of death, interacting with the divine, visiting the chamber of god, meeting deities and goddesses from various pantheons, and receiving initiations for several meditative practices.

Here are a few interesting examples of the potency of mushrooms:

Sergio is a Jewish man in his 40s. He loves his faith and goes to temple every Saturday morning with his children. He studies the Torah every week with friends. He does not wear a yarmulke but can definitely be considered a practicing Jew. In one of our sessions following his first mushroom journey with his guide, he told me, "I heard this song, and my body felt compelled to prostrate to the divine mother." The guide did not speak about the divine mother, nor was this a topic we had previously discussed. There was a song that played in the background that featured an Indian flute. Sergio proceeded to prostrate many times to the goddess and repeated a mantra. This was against his personal beliefs about the "right Jewish way to pray to god." This work was never intended to convert any individual from one belief system to another, but I do find that when people come and ask for a significant change in life, they often go through a process of ridding themselves of rigid belief systems. Consequently, they are better able to choose how they want to live their lives. Sergio did not stop going to temple or practicing Judaism, but his mind and heart opened up to allow devotion to enter his life and mind in ways that were less rigid and more accepting of other methods for connecting with the divine.

George is another interesting case. In his late 30s, divorced, and a father to three young boys, he also had only one kidney left, which was a donor kidney. Two years previously, George had spent four hours a day, three days a week, being hooked to a dialysis machine. His chances for a long life did not look very good. Yet, despite all the complications, surgeries, and recoveries, he did not experience any fear of death. He was, however, extremely heady and caught in loops of thoughts, worrying about money, the kids, the house, and how to better organize his schedule and belongings. In his second mushroom journey, he was finally ready to see how scared he was. The mushrooms "killed" him three times, and each time, he was reborn as a different species. One time he was born as a worm, then as a butterfly, then as a tree, and finally he returned to being human. Later, he told me, "I didn't even know I was scared of dying. I didn't even want to consider what it would mean for me and my children if I was to die." This experience did not cause George to be more fearful of death but rather to release a certain block that he had around this issue. The block required rigidity and coping, which had been causing the tight control that he asserted in his life.

The work with mushrooms can be a little bit uncertain. We have no idea what is going to come up, especially as the mushrooms tend to have a certain agenda for each journey. The fact that a specific individual usually reacts well to mushrooms does not mean that the next journey is going to be an easy one. Mushrooms are called los niños santos, the holy children. They are very powerful, and the more you take, the more power you give them to do their work.

In high doses, the individual usually remembers less, and the journey is along a much more spiritual path. The intensity of being high on mushrooms can be physically overwhelming due to the waves of energy that mushrooms bring into the psychic body. Ego dissolution can absolutely occur with mushrooms. So, anxiety and mushrooms do not work very well together, at least initially.

In addition, people who have more fragmented egos might get a lot more than they asked for. Friends are not appropriate sitters for them. Individuals with borderline personality disorder, for example, could be triggered in the middle of a journey and project an identity on a guide that is very far from reality. In some cases, people are known to become agitated and sometimes aggressive under the influence of mushrooms. In high dosages, it can become impossible or extremely hard to communicate with the user. Some people could finish the night in a police station or ER room. This only highlights the importance of having a highly experienced sitter or guide to be a ready support.

Psychedelic medicines in psychotherapeutic and guided settings can be very powerful vehicles for spiritual expansion, removal of energetic and psychological blocks, and teachings about the nature of self and reality. These tools are potent and should be used with caution and guidance. They are double-edged swords that can be extremely beneficial but also entail real risks and pitfalls. Always consult with experienced guides and doctors before pursuing medicine work yourself.

To conclude, I'd like to share a vision I received during a journey, offering insight into the benefits and obstacles central to medicine work.

Imagine a doorway before you. It resembles a saloon door with large, swinging panels. These doors can completely seal off the passage, or they can open wide, allowing you to pass through. Each door symbolizes a different domain of your being, a gateway to the various aspects of your life: memories, expectations, hopes, pain, worry, and pleasure.

Sometimes, these doors open on their own, moved by the winds that blow from outside. This could be an experience of loss, gaining money, someone coming for a surprise visit, or you fall in love. These are experiences that just happen to you. They open doors within you and you discover aspects of yourself that you never knew existed.

Other times, these doors open because of the wind that rises from within you; a sudden burst of creativity, a thought, a feeling of dread. When you look, when you gaze into a doorway, you send your own wind into it, influencing how it moves. You can decide to open a door, it is a shift that most people do unconsciously and following the natural wind of the mind. We have an ability to shift attention, to shift our gaze to a different thought stream, a topic, or an object of perception. You can sit in a temple and think about God or reflect on the concert from last night.

When we use medicine, it is like blowing an intense wind from the outside to force open a door. It is very effective. Sometimes people like the content of a domain that opens. Sometimes they like the act of opening the door which has a distinct feeling. Like going on a trip to Hawaii.

Medicine can force open a door and reveal a content, a domain, that previously was out-of-mind or out-of-reach. It can open a door to the divine, to memories, to fantasies, to the current events in your life, to many places.

However, the lock on the door remains closed unless you choose to open it. Sometimes, the wind created by substances can be so strong that it forces the doors open, compelling you to gaze into what lies beyond, to face and experience what is there. But remember, it is by your conscious choice alone that these doorways truly remain open, allowing information to flow freely. At the very least you learn to have relationships with these doors and have better access to them without having to force them open.

Once a door has been consciously opened, the use of external forces, like wind or substances, is no longer necessary to keep it open. The side effects, what we often refer to as 'getting high,' are merely temporary effects of using external means to open the door. These experiences, like everything else, pass in time. The advice of the medicine itself; "don't get attached to me."

As you continue the journey of diving deep into yourself, remember that the power to open and close these doors is within you. Return your gaze to the doorway of your choosing—whether it is love, money, power, the divine, pleasure, pain, and faith—they are all available to you, and each holds its own value.

And here's a gentle reminder: don't forget to turn back and look at the one who is looking.

Now, let's dive into one of the most important aspects of deep work—the integration of experiences emerging from meditative or psychedelic journeys.

Illustration 2: The Wheel of Life

CHAPTER 7

INTEGRATION

EXPERIENCES IN MEDITATION OR MEDICINE JOURNEYS CAN BE VERY powerful in one's evolution, particularly if there has been a shift in ego identity. However, the memory of these experiences tends to fade over time. Also, experiences remain experiences rather than translating into change if not integrated into our life. Without proper integration, many meditators and psychedelic users can be caught in a loop of chasing the next big experience (e.g., ego death, glimpses of the nature of mind, divine interactions, and so on) without applying the lessons of such experiences to the mechanics of their mind and into and out of their identity. In this chapter, I will review important aspects of integration and my model of how to apply deep work experiences to one's life.

The Wheel of Life

Illustration 2 is a depiction of the wheel of life, a photograph taken from Kopan Monastery in Budhanilkantha, Nepal, where I spent about six months in 2006. I present it here as a teaching about the importance of one's existence as a human birth and my understanding of the progression in psychospiritual integration.

Each element in this painting has an important symbolic meaning, but to facilitate the exposition, I will only describe a few.

The big red monster holding the wheel is called Yama, a wrathful deity who represents, among many things, impermanence. He is not evil, simply inevitable. Everything changes, including the rate of change itself. We have no escape from change, for better or worse.

At the innermost circle of the painting, the three animals represent the forces that keep the wheel of life (i.e., existence) rolling. The rooster represents greed (i.e., attachment to objects), the snake anger (i.e., avoidance or wanting to destroy objects), and the pig ignorance (i.e., of our true nature).

The next circle represents the movement of beings between various states of being, across bondage and increasing degrees of (spiritual) freedom.

The biggest and most important circle in this particular teaching depicts the six realms of beings. These beings could be taken literally as actual dimensions of reality that we do not see, something like the Olympus of Zeus and the hell realm of Hades. I describe each in detail in just a moment. Additionally, this teaching could be explained archetypally as the dimensions of a possible human existence. I connect better to the archetypal view, and in my opinion, we constantly move between these realms in our life, expressing different ways of being. We can spend parts of our life in one realm and then change into another. For example, I spent several years of my life in the cold hell and the animal realms before I was able to move into the human realm.

Let's start from the top and move clockwise:

THE GODS

The all-powerful people who have almost every possible power to do and live life as they wish. People like Elon Musk, Warren Buffet, and George Clooney. Yet, despite their enormous power, they live and die in time, even though they might get to live longer, given unlimited access to better health technologies and lifestyles. They are potentially addicted to bliss and freedom of choice and expression. Yet, like other beings, they do not escape suffering and pain. They will eventually lose their power and face death. Due to their immense freedom and power in life, their motivation to liberate themselves and seek out the truth of being is reduced. Most beings living in this realm end up moving into other realms sooner or later.

THE DEMIGODS

Very powerful humans who are endlessly hungry for power and more. They want to be gods, but this eludes them. They are drunk on power versus bliss and freedom, like Donald Trump, Putin, and Hitler. There is never enough, and they must get more. Their way is the only way. Their obsession with power destroys worlds and their own inner world. Liberation and the truth of being are not topics of interest to them.

HUNGRY GHOSTS

The people that live and die by a bottomless pit in their core. It does not matter how much food they eat, how much they drink, how much money they have, or how many clothes or cars they own. It is never enough. Their life energy is focused on accumulation and attempting to quench their soul's thirst. These are the Bernie Madoffs of our world, the addicts, and the compulsive Amazon buyers.

HELL

This realm describes humans controlled by one of two emotions: fear (the cold realm on the bottom right) or anger (the hot hell on the bottom left). Such individuals spend significant portions of their lives coping with fear and trying to get out of situations that cause this feeling. Or this could represent people who are subjected to anger, which lands them in difficult situations (e.g., prison, dissolution of relationships) or who spend enormous amounts of psychic energy keeping anger at bay.

ANIMALS

These are the majority of humans living in the world. They are enslaved by survival needs. They live day-to-day, searching for food, money, shelter, and medicines for their family members. They work all day, and once they are done, they usually spend the rest of their time taking care of loved ones. Most people living this life engage in spirituality as a religious practice in which they give their power to the clergy or god, wishing for a better outcome after death (e.g., going to heaven or having a more favorable reincarnation). There is no time or mental space in which exploration of the nature of reality is possible.

HUMANS

The human realm describes a life in which one has to work and survive but there is also enough time, space, safety, and resources to stop for a minute and ask the questions "Why am I here?" "What is the meaning of this life?" and "Who am I truly?" Unfortunately, most humans living in this realm are not motivated to ask these questions. Instead, they are focused on trying to make sure they do not fall into one of the other lower realms or on ascending to the higher realms (e.g., how do I get rich, famous, and powerful).

I see the purpose of therapy and medicine as helping us move from phases of life that are controlled by fear, anger, addiction, and insatiable hunger into the human realm, where there is more stability and freedom to live life as it is, without being bound by our conditioning. The Buddhist perspective considers the human realm to be an auspicious birth and encourages us to do all in our power to seek liberation. This involves getting off the wheel by finding for ourselves what reality truly is.

Nonlinear Progression

I see integration as conceptually divided into two types: preliminary and advanced. In the preliminary stage, the focus is on getting to the human realm and stabilizing our existence there. The only way to get there is to go through and not around. More specifically, this path is not about escape but rather experience. The only way toward psychospiritual evolution is to go deeply into our experience and initially be willing to experience it.

If we find ourselves in hell, then let's get intimate with it and find the way to another portion of the wheel. Many people who come to see me are "stuck" in a hell made out of fear or anger (i.e., in cases of severe abuse and complex trauma), while others are stuck in the hungry ghosts stage (i.e., in cases of addiction). After an individual can find some peace back in the human realm, they might end their journey there, and some might find spontaneous motivation to seek total liberation and get off the wheel.

Most people are not interested in enlightenment, and that is absolutely okay. But for some, after they begin to understand how deep the rabbit hole goes, a spark of interest could be ignited that, over time, will grow into a relentless fire that will not rest until the truth and nothing but the truth is revealed.

Commonly, integration is understood as the process of incorporating insights and experiences from psychedelic journeys or meditative experiences into our daily life. If you read a little further between the lines, it means bringing something from out there (i.e., spirituality, divine realms, journey space) into here (i.e., our default life) in an attempt to create positive changes in one's identity.

While this is progress in the right direction, at some point, this view can be seen for what it is: a self-referential movement in the service of the ego. In advanced integration, one will ultimately see that even spirituality is in the service of the ego. There is no other place out there or deep inside that is different from the words you are reading right now. Our bodies, the air we breathe, the thoughts we have, the terrible things we see on the news, and the clouds in the sky are all one. You can call it the body of god, the Self, or a strawberry pie; it does not matter. True and final integration means a permanent shift in identification from "I am here, separated from all, and am taking a journey to improve myself" to a deeper space of being: "I and all aspects of reality are one. The imperfect me and the perfect me are all one. Movement and stillness are one, and beyond it, the true nature of reality is ineffable." This is the Great Perfection.

Accessing and adapting to the truth of being is the work of advanced integration, which has a different focus, that of deep perceptual shifts and disidentification with the ego.

The progress from preliminary to advanced integration is not necessarily linear. I find in both my own case and those of others that there is a simultaneous process of integrating changes into our egoic identity and out of it. Change occurs over time for most people in a gradual manner.

Preliminary Integration

The focus in this type of work is on integrating experiences, visions, and insights from a journey or meditative experience into our egoic identity, and thus, gradually changing our ego.

Some of the experiences we have during journeys are life-altering in the moment they occur. This could be an insight or a somatic release. But many visions and downloads come and pass very quickly and can be forgotten. Many clients come back to me from a journey with multiple pages of notes that their guide transcribed during the time of their experience, attempting to record their insights and visions. They ask me, "What do I do now?"

I believe that, while working with the ego, the focus is to become intimate with it as much as we can. Awareness itself is the healer. It is the acid that melts the deposits, the oil that lubricates our parts, and the light that transforms the dark. Therefore, we want to create an intention and consider how we can enter into a more active relationship between the themes that come up in the journey space and our present daily life. Otherwise, the experiences will turn into conceptual insights (i.e., "talk the talk but not walk the walk"), merely an interesting topic for a dinner conversation, or worse, forgotten for a long period of time, wherein we miss the real opportunity of these experiences to change our lives.

Integration has no timeline. There are journeys that can take years to integrate, as some experiences unfold and develop into an understanding across an entire lifespan. The face of god, ancestral evolution, and having a multi-gender identity across various lifetimes—these are not things one can perceive *and* understand in one session.

Integration can be tricky. As a guide and therapist, you have to be creative, attentive, strategic, and brave to motivate others to engage in behaviors that contradict their default ego position. This is even more powerful in group integration, where there is amplification resulting from other eyes watching and communicating with the client.

I find two main ingredients facilitate successful integration of psychospiritual experiences into life: openness to change and embodiment.

Some clients come and ask for improvement in symptoms of depression or anxiety but do not actually want to change their belief system or life habits. They often view the journey or meditation as an isolated experience that will "cure" them like a psychotropic medication. Such individuals, and I see many, are not interested in doing much work themselves. With these clients, integration may not have much effect, as all guidance and discussion never leave the room. The concepts discussed remain thoughts or ideas. With these clients, I spend the majority of the time homing in on their resistance to change (with the intention of loosening the resistance) and less on integration itself.

With clients already open to change, I focus primarily on translating experience into life through action and behavior. One of the easiest ways to translate a cognitive insight or a feeling into a change of life is *embodiment*, that is, the conversion of vision, insight, and feeling into action and form. Embodiment practices often begin in sessions with a guide or therapist, and later, the client learns to practice more independently at home. This is because when embodiment is exercised in the presence of a witness, it is acknowledged and much more likely to grow roots and become a new habit.

EXAMPLES OF EMBODIMENT

INSIGHT	EMBODIMENT
Take care of myself	Make the bed and massage your own feet in sessions while voicing words of appreciation to your body.
Be kind to others	Start with a plant. I'll often ask a client to water a plant in my office with intention or to say kind words to it.
Be kind to myself	Turn your phone off in sessions (quite amazing how hard it is for us to disengage from our phones). Eat better. Light a candle and say a prayer for yourself.
Stop drinking	Make a ceremony in the room with sage and a cup of water to seal this idea into a commitment. Tell others about it or find an AA or SMART Recovery group. I might even give the client the number of an available sponsor on the spot.

Be more playful and lighter in life	Engage in a simple game in sessions or make funny faces to each other. My guide engaged me in a simple imaginative acting game when a memory of myself playing Dungeons and Dragons in my youth came up in a journey.
We are not separated—if one has had a non-dual, non-separated state of consciousness.	Change the way you speak to others in accordance with the view that we are not separated. Consider how you would treat the plants in your backyard or a homeless person if you are not separated. Meditate on what it is like for the clouds, sun, and you to all be one.
I am love—if one has had a non-dual state of love	Feel your heart space and demonstrate acts of love. Give hugs, write cards, and send warm energy and positive thoughts to others.

Embodied integration can also include nonverbal modalities. This can be very beneficial for a few personas: people who struggle to verbalize their experiences, individuals who tend to be hyperverbal and can benefit from learning other languages of expression, especially in connection with the body, and advanced journeyers and meditators who have learned that conceptual understanding is limited and are interested in nonverbal integration. Nonverbal integration is especially powerful when working with nondual paradoxes.

Nonverbal modalities can include working with clay, painting, dancing, making voices and sounds, singing, acting out particular movements, etc.

EXAMPLES OF INTEGRATION

The power of psychedelic medicines is that they allow more flexibility in people's thinking, feelings, and behaviors. This is often referred to as neuroplasticity. The two weeks following a psychedelic experience are a golden opportunity to bring change into people's minds and habits, as there seems to be a decrease in psychological resistance to change.

Erin, a female in her 50s, showed resistance to meditation throughout two years of psychotherapy. One MDMA journey with her guide opened her up to including meditation as a daily morning ritual. During the journey, she had a powerful experience of feeling deep into her body and identifying several undigested emotional experiences. The day following the journey, in a one-on-one integration session, she was able to meditate with the therapist and then later began to repeat the same practice immediately upon waking up.

This new habit lasted about three months. Even though Erin's ego patterns came back, the "damage" was done. A devout software engineer and atheist who previously refused to even discuss meditation, she was able, on frequent occasions, to "go inside" and meet unknown aspects of herself. Her identity was forever shifted. Like a big ocean liner, just a slight shift in the helm can change the course of one's life and affect the lives of thousands.

Integration is not always about how to become someone new or embody positive insights in our life. Often, especially in working with trauma, integration focuses on processing deep and difficult emotions that were previously locked away.

Robert, a male in his late 30s, married and a father to two young children, was severely physically abused and neglected by his parents. He came into therapy with deep depression, anxiety, and rage attacks that he found very difficult to control.

Although he knew about his trauma, his first and second MDMA journeys revealed the depths and magnitude of locked emotions, knots in his psychic and physical body, and exiled psychological parts (a five-year-old who was locked in a completely dark closet as a punishment). For Robert, the emergence of the visceral experience of fear, anger, shame, and pain during these journeys was overwhelming. However, the protective mechanisms of the ego that had kept him alive and facilitated his mental survival for most of his life were causing too much collateral damage, and he had no choice but to reveal his innermost parts. Therefore, his integration following the journey had to focus on allowing emotional experience while balancing being overwhelmed.

Journaling and individual or group therapy can be helpful in such cases, but often, more somatic and expressive interventions are needed. These could include working with a punching bag, screaming into a pillow or in a car, falling to the ground in helpless sobs, painting with your entire body, working with clay, or anything that facilitates the muscle of "allowing." For someone who has never had permission to do so, beginning can be overwhelming. Some clients described it as "like someone connected me to a firehose and turned it full on for several days and weeks following the journey."

In my case, I can share that it took me a year and a half to teach my body and psyche that it was now allowed to feel and experience emotions to a fuller extent. There were periods of anger, crying, and shame spirals. Work sometimes also needs to be done with family members to help them understand what the individual is going through and create a safe environment where there is a balance between free expression and others' physical and psychological safety and needs.

Once permission is given to the experience and expression of difficult emotions and exiled psychological parts, access to positive emotions and experiences is generally enhanced. This is often referred to as the gold in the shadow. Once Robert was able to connect with and experience his fear, anger, and shame, he could also remember that, once in a while, his father would buy him ice cream and that his mother would apologize to him and sing him lullabies. He could remember that his parents did love him despite the abuse. Following that understanding, forgiveness and letting go became possible, even if they were still further down the road.

Jay was a handsome guy in his early 30s, financially successful, yet with limited ability to strike lasting romantic relationships with women, despite his desire to start a family. Overall, he felt lonely in life, even though he had some friends. He looked great and had money, good social skills, and no major trauma.

Jay participated in a powerful group psilocybin mushroom journey. This is a modality in which individuals take mushrooms together in a guided ceremonial setting. Although each individual does their work separately on their own mat, the assumption (and my subjective experience) is that the presence of a group amplifies the effects of the medicine and also acts as an intervention in itself. The following day, the group members usually integrate their experiences in a group-process format.

The main theme the journey took for Jay was "grow up and start taking care of yourself." During group integration following the journey, he was asked to identify a simple way to demonstrate taking care of himself. He identified "making his bed" as an applicable activity he could focus on every day to embody and remember his commitment to this insight. As a response to Jay's share, the guide threw a blanket and a pillow in disarray on the floor and asked Jay to "make his bed." Jay could not do so because he immediately sank to the floor sobbing. The guide suggested Jay ask one of the other participants to help and teach him how to make his bed. Jay was able to choose one individual with whom he had a close empathetic connection, and after that individual ceremonially showed him how, he was able to then make his bed. This all ended in a loving group hug that further cemented the relationship between "taking care of myself," connection with others, and positive feeling.

POTENTIAL PITFALLS OF INTEGRATION

The ego is an identity machine and will appropriate any new experience into our self-image. Therefore, there is a danger in this work of the ego establishing a new identity around the expression of difficult states and emotions. For example, in Robert's case, as anger rose to the surface and was given permission to express itself, there was also an egoic movement of appropriation claiming, "I am a monster!" This had to be addressed through psychoeducation and the release of that thought stream.

As in Robert's case, sometimes the release of trauma can overwhelm our physiology and psychology. I have seen people come back from journeys with intense experiences of sadness (e.g., in the case of a parent losing their child to suicide), shame (e.g., in the case of a mother abusing her children), and anger (e.g., in the case of a man raped by his grandfather). The release and experience of these emotions and the associated energetic shift can be so overwhelming that the clients could slip into retraumatization.

It is a delicate process to keep a balance between allowing experiences that facilitate release and not creating further psychological wounding that will take a great deal of time to recover from. As with physical exercise, stress on the muscles and bones is good and healthy for growth, but we do not want to overdo it to the point of sustaining a stress injury that needs to be healed and thus prevents us from engaging in further exercise.

The choice of when to pause the process of unfolding should be made in collaboration with the client, guide, therapist, and the client's support system. Pausing the unfolding could be done via distraction, energy work, or a vacation, but sometimes psychotropic medications might need to be revisited, at least for a while.

Suzie, a prominent leader in the business community, came into treatment with what appeared to be a relatively mild case of parental neglect. Her goal was to be better connected with the divine. However, following one MDMA journey with her guide, she began spiraling with unexpected, consecutive daily panic attacks that disabled her from functioning as a mother, spouse, and business leader. Psychotherapy and the use of coping skills were ineffective against her panic and rising anxiety, and eventually, a mild antipsychotic was the only thing that enabled her to calm down. Within four months, she was able to discontinue the antipsychotic and return to deep work. Ultimately, her experience was extremely beneficial, as it brought up deep existential fears that stood between her and a connection with the divine.

Advanced Integration

Darius, a beautiful man in his 40s, was paying dearly for an affair he had become involved in about a year before walking into my office. He had lost his job and house, his kids did not want to see him anymore, and his wife was about to become his ex.

"This is not the life I wanted! There is no job out there that will pay enough for the kind of life I want to have. I want freedom!"

Darius was seeking freedom to live his life the way he wanted. I was not able to give him that. Maybe Tony Robbins could. What I could do was help

Darius find the freedom to live his life as it is. Many individuals find this notion unnerving, as they want their circumstances to change. For Darius, it was reflected in his words, "I don't want to become my grandfather. He gave up on life and let it decide for him, and he got nothing out of it. My discipline and willpower made me into who I am." It did not take long to demonstrate the ruins of his life to remind him that self-discipline and will-power have their inevitable limits.

The freedom to live life *as it is* is the freedom to feel our emotions as they arise without bracing or stopping them. It means the freedom to experience the inner and outer world without chronic contraction. Thoughts, desires, and fantasies are permitted. You increase your ability to take joy in the flowers surrounding you, smell the dog poop you stepped on, bury your father, cry in your mother's embrace, savor the dance of lovemaking, lick ice cream, birth your children, and die in your lover's arms. Are you free to live life in its entire spectrum? When do you say, "Stop! I don't want to feel this. I don't want to experience this"? What's important is to bring awareness to this feeling and then make an intentional choice from a place of acceptance.

Advanced integration focuses on the capacity to meet life and live it as it is. It does not turn us into zombies or carpets that people walk on. On the contrary, we develop even better access to anger that comes out as natural feedback when someone irritates us. We also have the freedom to become annoyed, horny, achy, and have a bad case of resting bitch face. All is welcome. Life in its entirety is welcome.

The relaxation that we previously learned to meet with resistance has been integrated into our ego and body. Now, it is time to bring relaxation to the level of identification. Move the focus from what "I" want for "my life" to what life is in a continuous process of giving and receiving. What does life want to provide me with and ask of me? This requires developing a somatic familiarity and willingness to experience life as it is.

The question of free will arises here. Whether free will exists or not is irrelevant, and the question is nothing but a distraction. In this level of integration, you are asked to experiment with letting go of your free will by letting go of yourself. For some people, this comes because of severe pain—letting go of the self is the only way forward out of the immense suffering they live through on a daily basis. For others, this process can come more gradually and naturally. In both cases, some intention and personal work can go a long way to facilitate this transition.

In the beginning stages of a spiritual quest, there is a stark difference between journey spaces or meditative states and the default life. However, with time and practice, the boundary between *alternate* and *ordinary* conscious states weakens and gradually loses strength. Then, one sunny day, it absolutely disappears and never comes back, as one understands that they are a perfect appearance, cherished and loved in the endless loving presence that we are. Sometimes that just happens on the spot. It can happen at any moment, and it is a gift when given. It is not something you can grab and hold on to. It is an abiding awakening.

The vast majority of people on the spiritual path experience a gradual shift. This group includes people who have had glimpses of the nature of mind, spending sometimes weeks or months in alternate states of being but still eventually returning to at least a partial identification with the "me" story.

I want to emphasize that there is absolutely no rush to arrive at an abiding awakening. Wherever you are, it is perfect. You are going to make it. The speed depends on your motivation.

In the end, seeking itself becomes an aspect of identity that must be seen for what it is, a part of the "me" complex. The major motivators for most people at this point of pushing forward include the intense wish to be free of suffering and pain, wanting to experience reality as it is, desperately wanting to know "the truth," or becoming close and one with the divine.

EGO DEATH

For many psychedelic users and spiritual seekers, ego death is considered to be the holy grail of alternate states of consciousness. I think that the word "death" is somewhat confusing. In my experience, for most people, ego death is not as exotic as it sounds. The experience is better described as "ego pause."

The hallmark of that experience is the dissolution of ego boundaries, which can spontaneously lead to the experience of unity consciousness. That is a sense of oneness with the universe where there is no separation between "me" and the external world.

The dissolution of ego boundaries can be gradual, partial, gentle, or aggressive and complete. Meditation and several psychedelic medicines tend to make the process more gradual. For example, with ketamine, careful layering of the medicine and using gradual doses brings on a progressive cessation of perceived sensory input into consciousness. With this medicine, the less perception we have of our body, the fewer ego boundaries we have. With other medicines, such as mushrooms, DMT, and 5-MeO-DMT, the dissolution can be more difficult to control and is more likely to be sudden and aggressive.

I would compare the experience I had on 5-MeO-DMT as the closest death simulation I have ever had. For about 30 minutes (in clock time, although my subjective perception was of no time), I had no body, no thoughts, no perception, and no sense of me, just being. It was a very palatable experience, yet one difficult to articulate. Obviously, as the medicine wore off, I returned to my body in an experience that felt like rebirth. Naturally, the ego, which was on pause, returned as thoughts and intense feelings about the experience emerged: "Look what happened to ME!"

For the rare individual, even though the ego returns as the machine that makes us human (i.e., the production of language, discernment between hot and cold, etc.), the absolute identification with it does not return.

Therefore, what's important in the experience of ego death is not the cessation of the ego but seeing and experiencing that even when the ego stops (i.e., temporarily dies), consciousness continues. This experience assists in dislodging the tight identification that we have with the ego and the body. This subsequently permits us to stop fighting with the ego, allowing its presence in our life while, at the same time, we begin to identify with our true nature, supreme and total consciousness. This process is more gradual and permanent, leading to a perceptual shift rather than the "jumping" between states of "I got it!" and "Now I lost it!"

WORKING WITH PARADOX

One of the common phenomena in higher states of consciousness is the experience of paradox. This can occur both during a journey or meditation. An example is having the visceral experience of both being the absolute (such as total stillness) and the relative (being a small human running around the world in madness).

The entire psychedelic process is often a paradox, as in many medicines, you can still be present in the body while your consciousness is able to experience other, deeper, and more subtle dimensions of being.

I find the boundary between the present reality and other realities to be a very fertile ground in which to do our deep work. Medicine aficionados often like to let go of their body and travel far into higher realms. This may require rather high doses of medicine, which has advantages and disadvantages. The veil between the conscious and the unconscious is, in my opinion, where the magic happens. It is the space where energy turns into matter and collective unconscious streams of thoughts become our personal thoughts and imagination.

The human instinct is to resolve the paradox. As we live primarily in the dualistic world, the ego and conceptual mind do not appreciate states and thought patterns that cannot resolve or yield a final answer. However, once you start dabbling in this work, you will quickly come to realize that many existential questions do not have a final answer. The answer is often a paradox, which can become disorienting and distressing at times.

One personal, profound experience of paradox occurred during an MDMA journey. As the medicine came on, I found myself looking at myself as an embryo in my mother's uterus. I could also feel myself as the embryo. The entrée of the journey was the umbilical cord connecting my tiny and helpless body to my mother's. I was comfortable, warm, and protected. I was receiving love and nutrients through the umbilical cord and was safe in the somatic knowledge that all was provided. However, after some time,

I could feel other things flowing through the umbilical cord into my being: my mother's anger, fear, hate for men, and the buds of codependency that would later color our relationship. The intensity of these difficult emotions grew larger and deeper. The embryo had no understanding of what it was he was experiencing. He reacted with instinct and confusion to the mixed signals coming through the umbilical cord. There were love and nutrients, but also toxins and terror. There was no escape. The embryo was helpless when trying to get away from a source of love and pain. "Let me out!" was the scream echoing in my awareness, but no one was listening other than my adult consciousness having this experience now.

With time, insights began to pour out. The journey developed into the perception of the paradox of love. As I experienced it in the uterus, this was about the polarity of love and betrayal. The people who love us the most, who nourish us the most, are also the ones who betray us sooner or later. They turn their love away to themselves or in other directions that ask for that love. Our beloved also have their pain and suffering, and our bond of love is a channel that allows all emotions and sensations to flow back and forth in a feedback loop.

I wanted to resolve this paradox in the journey. But there was no final answer. How do you live a life of love without experiencing betrayal on the receiving or giving end? There was no answer. More than that, how do you settle love and betrayal with the beloved itself (i.e., the divine)? My ego, despite its best efforts, could not resolve this. It was distressing on somatic and cognitive levels. However, thanks to my guide and a previous acquaintance with paradox, I was able, at some point, to surrender. Once I did, I could perceive and experience that there was no need to resolve the paradox. Rather, the paradox enabled the fabric of physical reality, of duality, of relationships in themselves. There is no relationship without duality. There is no love without betrayal, no bliss without pain. And alternatively, there is no pain without bliss, and every betrayal is a demonstration of love.

"Duh," one might say. I recognize the cliché nature of this realization, but to experience this philosophical truth on a somatic, perceptual level was a life-changing moment that I wish for all.

Language and concepts that belong to the dualistic world cannot resolve paradoxes that combine nondual and dual realities. Your body, however, can do much better. Language cannot say "love and betrayal" at the same time. But your hands can symbolize them both at the same moment. In an ordinary state of consciousness, this will mean nothing, but in an extra-conscious state (through medicine or meditation), this can become a mode of processing and understanding on a deep level that bypasses the limited cognitive conceptual level. It is a deep form of knowing that can later be somewhat expressed on the conceptual level.

THE FOLDING OF CONSCIOUSNESS

The following is my own interpretation from Genesis (1:26): "And God said, Let *Us* make humankind in our image and our shadow . . ." (the original verse: "Then God said, let Us make man in Our image, according to Our likeness;")

> If I had to give a geometric perspective on the nature of consciousness, then the absolute is a point of singularity or, further still, no point in no space. There is no geometry for the total absolute. There is basically really nothing you can say about it accurately.

> However, in the relative state of consciousness that humans experience, consciousness is geometrically folded onto itself. We experience this day-to-day as self-referential thoughts and egoic movements. Imagine you were the sun, blazing rays of light, and consider these rays shortly after leaving the center, bending back towards the center. These rays of light (which represent our thoughts, sensations, and perceptions) are "obsessed" with trying to sense the origin from which they came. Of course, this is impossible, like an eyeball trying to see itself without a mirror or a dog chasing its tail. For the eye to see itself, it must use a mirror (which is why the creation of "other" sets of eyes occurred).

> The visceral experience of the folding of consciousness is somewhat similar to what the human brain looks like when you open up a skull. There

are many folds. It is folded onto itself, which serves a neurological purpose. During medicine journeys (especially with mushrooms), there is often a visceral feeling to the folded nature of reality and consciousness. This can be disorienting and nauseating at times, especially on high dosages of psilocybin, often becoming an experience that journeyers would like to move away from.

However, I recommend working on opening yourself up to this experience, as there is much to learn from it. In Dzogchen, and especially the Longdé (body and energy) series, there is an emphasis on learning how to extend our energy channels, like a radiating star whose rays are completely extended and not curving back on themselves. This requires disengaging from self-reference: "How am I doing?" "Am I doing this right?" "Did I get it?" "Did I lose it?" "Who am I?" "What am I?" and so on and so forth.

What is it like to cease self-referencing in our ordinary lives? Notice the resistance in the mind and body to this suggestion (egoic defense). Is it even possible? It is! The thought stream might still be there, but identification with it does not need to occur. As we go further and further into deep work, identification disengages, the power behind self-reference diminishes, and one can more freely live and experience reality as it is: as a pure and dynamic being.

The Dream Machine

I will end with a story I once heard from Christopher Wallis. Here is my version of it: Imagine yourself to be a divine being, capable of creating and doing anything, except dying. You are limitless. You create kingdoms and worlds. You take pleasure in it all, to the deepest depths. You try everything sensually, sexually, energetically, materially, and spiritually. It is mahanirvana, total heaven.

But at some point, you get bored. All imagination becomes tasteless, as all content within it has one underlying taste: you.

One day, strolling down the street or flying on a red dragon, a machine appears. The writing on the front panel says, "Dream Machine. Push the red button to dive into your wildest dream ever. No restrictions. Absolute surprise guaranteed! Devour your biggest passions, darkest terrors, and crushing loves. Terror guaranteed! Sex guaranteed! Love guaranteed! Life guaranteed!"

Then some very fine print at the end of that text says, "Please note: the above requires total forgetfulness, and you will forget your true identity. Side effects can include panic, terror, psychosis, intense pain, grief, and migraines. As nothing in the universe is permanent, this machine comes with a self-expired timer. Upon reaching 8,276,911 reiterations of the dream, it will begin to naturally dissipate. We believe in slow and natural awakening for our clients. Nothing like a nice morning snooze. Please note, this number could shift based on the user's willingness to continue the dream if satisfaction is achieved. Have a nice day."

The question is not whether you will press the button but when.

Do you remember your true nature?

Would you like to know?

CONCLUSION

A FEW DAYS AFTER JOE'S JOURNEY WITH MUSHROOMS, HE CAME TO MY office for an integration session and to discuss his experiences. His guide had instructed him to wait a few days and let the experience unfold spontaneously and not to analyze or conceptualize the journey, as words could not really provide an appropriate container for what he experienced.

"I don't know what to do now. I was confronted with the infinite to such a degree that my entire life has been put into question. My first journey was like watching a movie about the behind the scenes of reality; in the second journey, I died and was reborn as many others; and in the third, I became the infinite, no longer witnessing as an observer but realizing that I am the Infinite. And now, here I am sitting with you. Now what?"

To me, this story symbolizes the observation that there is never really an end or final snapshot to life. The end is nothing but a conceptual construct. Reality and life appear to be a continuous stream of consciousness, with ebbs and flows, highs and lows. It is the human mind that attempts to take snapshots and name them "beginning" and "end," but those are nothing but single frames in an infinite movie. In summary, evolution is ongoing, and the journey continues as consciousness unfolds. In self-development, there will be moments when the focus shifts from "how to live" to "living life." But the teachings and flowering of consciousness are never complete. There will always be another mountain, a new shadow, or a lesson to learn. What could come to an end is the search and hunger for a final solution that will make one perfect. For each person, the puzzle is unique and surprising. I wish for you to engage in this process with curiosity, passion, and joy.

Despite the darkness prevalent in our world today—wars, geopolitical conflicts, hunger, inequality, and the silencing and terrorizing of segments of the population—there is also an apparent wave of human psychological and spiritual evolution currently taking place, which appears to be accelerating.

When I was a child, there was little access to teachers and settings that promoted free spiritual and psychological expansion. The freedom and psychological safety available in many Western countries today are comparable with the wave of Renaissance flourishing in Europe in the 14th century. Today, the internet and the flowering of teachers in the West have created better access to learning and the practice of self-development techniques. These include meditation, mindfulness, emotional intelligence, yoga, tai chi, and so on. Furthermore, psychedelic teachers have formed an undeniable bridgehead in our societies and moved from being solely among indigenous groups and isolated practitioners into mainstream culture. The slow process of legalization of some psychedelic substances has promoted research, and their use has increased in prominent medical and mental health treatment settings in addition to forming a symbiotic relationship with spiritual expansion.

In summary, due to the improved access to nondual teachings, teachers, and psychedelic substances, powerful psychospiritual experiences are much more prevalent at this point in time than probably ever before in human history. This is a double-edged sword. It is a tremendous gift to humanity that can assist us in transitioning from our current global civilization into a new phase of inner and outer exploration that will propel us into uncharted territories. Yet, there is the danger that irresponsible use and basic misunderstanding of such deep teachings can trap us in loops of suffering and confusion. In order for us to support a more positive shift for humanity and the rest of life on this planet, we can all, at the very least, engage openheartedly in an individual process of evolution that could also translate into a collective evolution.

A process of personal evolution that relies on psychological approaches alone, although life-changing, is usually frustratingly slow and prone to substantial setbacks. Often, it is just a matter of time before relapse occurs or another set of problems emerges. Ultimately, mental health problems and stagnation in our civilization are existential in nature and not psychological. People can benefit from taking their self-development to the next level by focusing on.

This involves understanding that spirituality is an integral part of self-development and the betterment of mankind. This does not require one to become religious in any way but to simply open oneself to subjective experiences that go beyond science, dogma, and conceptual understanding.

The primary arc of this process entails self-discovery rather than fixing oneself. The more intimate we become with our deepest parts, the more we can realize our true nature. Such a realization and intimacy spontaneously lift the basic misunderstanding humans have of reality. When we become increasingly aware of our true nature, we can come in touch with the divine nature of reality. Suffering and pain make sense when seen in the context of the true nature of reality; the path to liberation becomes simple, as we can see our misunderstanding more clearly; and the fruit of awakening becomes more tangible.

Deep work can be more effective, and pitfalls are better avoided, if one can spend time shaping and training several fundamental skills. These include attention training and developing the ability to see and work with thoughts: how they arise, remain in stasis, and then dissolve. Developing an ability to witness the space in which thoughts arise is most important. In addition, it is important to find guides, teachers, and a community who can support us in this process. Deep work is safest and most potent when done with robust community support.

Deep work relies on a better understanding of what the ego (i.e., identity) is and how it operates. More specifically, what are our ego defenses and their course of action? As we better understand the ego and its fundamental characteristics, we stop being lost in it and feel more in harmony with life. We can become liberated from conditioning and the momentum of thinking, feeling, and behaving that has directed us for a very long time. With time and practice, the ego also stops being our nemesis and turns into an old friend invested in our survival and happiness. We can live side by side as our identity shifts. As one dives deeper into the work, it is important to understand and experience shifts in identity. This means being able to connect with intimacy, acceptance, and love for our deepest parts: our inner child, exiled identities, protectors, firefighters, and other exotic and esoteric personalities.

As one works with thoughts and identities, the ability to develop a new perspective on pain and suffering is crucial. More specifically, being able to see pain and suffering in the larger context of life, understanding their crucial role in evolution, and being able to tolerate discomfort without immediately having to resolve it. Deep work requires both understanding and working with the body-mind complex. More specifically, understanding and working with the psychic body and energetic phenomena are crucial for human evolution and the treatment of mental health disorders. This includes learning and working with the chakra system and meridians, as well as understanding samskaras and energetic manipulation using meditation, touch, and medicine work. It is important to overcome the resistance that mainstream science and Western culture have to energetic phenomena. Yes, we cannot currently measure psychic energy or see it with our own eyes, but that does not mean we cannot use it or develop models of reality that accept energy as a fundamental process of the human body and psyche. Similarly, we cannot see the quantum dimension with our own eyes, yet it is a fundamental part of electronic components.

Success in deep work requires an ability to connect with our body and develop a healthy and intimate relationship with both our physical and energetic bodies in a curious, open, and compassionate manner.

Deep work, for many people, incorporates psychedelic medicines as powerful allies and tools. These entheogenic substances can be very beneficial in human development, mental health treatment, and spiritual expansion. Psychedelics can be powerful teachers, bringing insights. They can introduce us to alternate states of consciousness, demonstrating how complex and interdimensional reality actually is. Psychedelic teachers can also be forces of healing, primarily focusing on the energetic and somatic healing of the psychic body.

Nevertheless, there are risks in working with psychedelic medicine and deep meditative states. The use of these substances is not for everyone, and they should be approached with caution. More specifically, one must be attentive to the possibilities of psychological dependency, new processes of egoic identification, and physiological and psychological stress. As the use of psychedelics becomes more prolific in our society, one must be cautious about choosing the right guide, setting, and processes to support the individual journey. Be wary of the dangers of venturing deep into yourself and the nature of reality without appropriate support.

To be better able to work with psychedelic medicine or deep meditative states, an important foundation is the ability to experience extra-conscious states (e.g., out-of-body experiences, ego dissolution, synesthesia, downloading, and channeling) without getting lost in the content of such experiences. As such states can be overwhelming, super-intriguing, and ego-syntonic, individuals often lose themselves in the content or form new identities around their experiences. Familiarity with such states helps individuals to remain grounded in the nature of being while being able to leap and dissolve into these experiences.

Lastly, deepening our evolution relies on understanding the nature of resistance as the ego's protective strategy; learning to relate to it with a gentle, loving attitude; and finding specific ways to relax into our deepest nature.

Deep work and any form of personal development are incomplete without proper integration. Integration can be theoretically viewed as divided into preliminary and advanced stages. Preliminary integration focuses on incorporating insights and experiences into our current egoic identity, while advanced integration focuses on perceptual shifts that gradually give birth to a version of ourselves beyond our regular egoic identification.

Samsara is infinite, and if one only targets the superficial layers of being, one will remain stuck in cycles of pain and suffering their entire life. More specifically, we can become hypnotized for many years by discovering additional samskaras, psychological parts, and self-images. Following the initial awakening and lessening of self-images and samskaras, I believe the focus needs to eventually shift to realizing our true nature and viscerally experiencing our true identity.

Advanced integration ultimately entails the understanding that all tools need to be relinquished, including meditation and medicine. This does not mean that we have to stop engaging with meditation or medicine but that we stop being dependent on these tools for our awakening and evolution.

WHAT NOW?

Keep going, do not stop, and forever follow your inner compass. There are phases in life in which there will be pauses in your expansion. At the end of the day, a good life relies on a balance between exploring nature and the self and living life as it comes to us.

Find a teacher, go to therapy, read spiritual books, join or create a spiritual community, attend a meditation retreat, find new perspectives through which to view reality, and explore. Eventually, you will find your own way. I stand on the shoulders of giants but reach into the skies with my own hands. Others will be supported by whatever I can offer. Take your place and find your destiny.

Your path is likely to include as many lows as highs. I have never had a teacher who did not disappoint me. A client once told me, "You should never have a beer with your hero." Once you hit a pitfall or a very dark spot, allow yourself to experience the moment, the darkness and disappointment. Then, when the movement of emotion seems to liberate itself, reach for the next bar and allow life to pull you onwards.

I wish you a sweet dive into your essence. May your wishes and heart's desire fulfill themselves, for the benefit of all.

RESOURCES

T HE FOLLOWING ARE BOOKS AND OTHER SOURCES OF INFORMATION THAT I found to be very beneficial in my self-development and psychospiritual journey. There are many others, but this is a great start.

SPIRITUALITY, EGO, CONSCIOUSNESS, THE NATURE OF REALITY, MEDITATION:

Falling into Grace by Adyashanti

Inner Engineering by Sadhguru

Tantra Illuminated by Christopher Wallis

The End of Your World by Adyashanti

The Recognition Sutras by Christopher Wallis

The Supreme Source by Namkhai Norbu

Tibetan Book of Living and Dying by Sogyal Rinpoche

True Meditation by Adyashanti

When Things Fall Apart by Pema Chödrön

Who Am I? by Sri Ramana Maharshi

PSYCHOLOGICAL PROCESSES, EGO, THE UNCONSCIOUS, AND RESISTANCE:

Homecoming by John Bradshaw

Inner Work by Robert Johnson

No Bad Parts by Richard Schwartz

Owning Your Own Shadow by Robert Johnson

The Body Keeps the Score by Bassel van der Kolk

The Ethics of Caring by Kylea Taylor

A great resource I recommend to learn about and work with resistance is Milton Erickson's writing and instructional videos, all available for purchase at *https://catalog.erickson-foundation.org/*

PSYCHIC OR ENERGY BODY:
Awakening Kundalini by Lawrence Edwards
In Touch by John Prendergast
The Deep Heart by John Prendergast
"The Real Story on the Chakras" by Christopher Wallis (https://medium.com/@hareesh_59037/the-real-story-on-the-chakras-b321fd662daa)

PSYCHEDELICS AND MEDICINE:
Consciousness Medicine by Françoise Bourzat
Food of the Gods by Terence McKenna
How to Change Your Mind by Michael Pollan
The Cosmic Game by Stanislav Grof
The Psychedelic Explorer's Guide by James Fadiman

GENERAL SHAMANISM AND ENGAGEMENT WITH NATURE:
Plant Spirit Medicine by Eliot Cowan
The Way of the Shaman by Michael Harner

www.ingramcontent.com/pod-product-compliance
Lightning Source LLC
Chambersburg PA
CBHW071218090426
42736CB00014B/2874